Contents

EDEXCEL

GCSE Modern World History

REVISION GUIDE

Steve Waugh and Ben Walsh

HODDER
EDUCATION

Acknowledgements

Photo credits
p.104 © The body of a German telephone operator in his shelter at the Somme, 1916 (b/w photo) by Moreau, Jacques (b.1887) Archives Larousse, Paris, France/ Giraudon/The Bridgeman Art Library; **p.107** 'The Kitchen Is The Key To Victory, Eat Less Bread', 1st World War poster, c.1917 (colour litho), English School, (20th century)/Private Collection, Barbara Singer/The Bridgeman Art Library; **p.120** © Getty Images; **p.122** © The National Archives/HIP/TopFoto; **p.135** © Jackson Daily News/Fred Blackwell/AP/Press Association Images; **p.137** © Getty Images.

Every effort has been made to contact copyright holders, and the publishers apologise for any omissions which they will be pleased to rectify at the earliest opportunity.

Although every effort has been made to ensure that website addresses are correct at time of going to press, Hodder Education cannot be held responsible for the content of any website mentioned in this book. It is sometimes possible to find a relocated web page by typing in the address of the home page for a website in the URL window of your browser.

Hachette UK's policy is to use papers that are natural, renewable and recyclable products and made from wood grown in sustainable forests. The logging and manufacturing processes are expected to conform to the environmental regulations of the country of origin.

Orders: please contact Bookpoint Ltd, 130 Milton Park, Abingdon, Oxon OX14 4SB. Telephone: (44) 01235 827720. Fax: (44) 01235 400454. Lines are open 9.00–5.00, Monday to Saturday, with a 24-hour message-answering service. Visit our website at www.hoddereducation.co.uk.

© Steve Waugh and Ben Walsh.

First published in 2010 by Hodder Education,
An Hachette UK company,
338 Euston Road,
London NW1 3BH

Impression number   5 4 3 2 1
Year   2013 2012 2011 2010

Cover photo: Civil Rights Marchers with 'I Am A Man' Signs © Bettmann/CORBIS
Illustrations by Barking Dog Art, Peter Lubach and Phoenix Photosetting
Typeset in 11.5/13.5 Garamond by Phoenix Photosetting, Chatham, Kent ME4 4TZ
Printed in Spain

A catalogue record for this title is available from the British Library

ISBN: 978 0340 992 210

Introduction

You will soon be taking your GCSE in Modern European and World History. Your aim is to get the best grade that you can. Our aim in this book is to help you get that grade.

To improve your grade you need to:
- get organised – this book will help you make a revision plan and stick to it
- know the content – this book will help you learn the core content for your course
- apply your knowledge – this book will help you apply what you know to actual examination questions.

How to revise

There is no single way to revise, but there are some golden rules everyone should follow.

1 *Know the objectives of your course:* ask your teacher for full details of the specification. This book is geared to Edexcel's specification A, Modern European and World History.
2 *Make a revision plan and stick to it:* start your revision early – the earlier the better. Revise regularly – regular, short spells are better than panicky six-hour slogs until 2a.m.
3 *Revise actively:* be a scribbler; make notes as you learn. You will need an exercise book for most of the Revision Tasks but you can also write in this book.

The rest of this introduction is about how to apply these rules to your revision and make sure that you get the grade you are aiming for.

1. Know the objectives of your course

Assessment objectives for GCSE History

1 *Recall, select and communicate knowledge and understanding of history.*
   You have to be able to recall and select knowledge, and be able to communicate it in a way that shows you understand what you are writing.
   This means:
- using your knowledge of a topic to back up what you say in your answer
- organising this knowledge to answer the question that has been set.

2 *Demonstrate understanding of the past through explanation and analysis of:*
- *key concepts: causation, consequence, continuity, change and significance within a historical context*
- *key features and characteristics of the periods studied and the relationship between them.*

   This means organising your answer in order to:
- show the ability to analyse when this is asked for, rather than to describe
- show understanding of causation, etc.

3 Understand, analyse and evaluate:
   (a) a range of source material as part of an historical enquiry
   This means using any kind of material, including photographs, diaries, books, recorded interviews and films from the period you are studying.

   You are expected to:
- extract what is important information from the source
- interpret what is being said and make inferences
- decide how useful or reliable the source is.

(b) how aspects of the past have been interpreted and represented in different ways as part of an historical enquiry

This means that you have to be able to analyse and interpret how and why historical events, people and situations have been interpreted and represented in different ways.

You are expected to:
- decide how fair or accurate an interpretation is
- compare different representations of an event.

In all this, remember that the examiner is interested in seeing how much you can think for yourself and apply your knowledge and understanding to the question set.

2. Make a revision plan

You not only need to plan your revision for History, but you need to fit it in with the revision for all your other GCSE subjects. You could use this table to plan your overall revision.

Dates		Revision targets and deadlines			
Month	Week	History	Science	English	Others
Jan	4	Key points summary card for Russia			
Feb	2		Test on metals		
Mar				Controlled Assessment session	

You could then construct another table, like the one below, to plan your History revision. In your plan, aim to come back to each topic several times so that you revise in stages:

Stage 1: Put the date that normal school-based work on a topic is due to be/was completed.
Stage 2: Put the target date for finishing your own summary of the key points for each topic.
Stage 3: Decide when you will give yourself memory tests.
Stage 4: Schedule time for fine-tuning your revision (for example, final memorising work and/or practice examination questions).

History topics	Date	Key points summary	Memory test	Fine tuning
1 Stalin's Five-Year Plans		March	April	2000 Question–May
2 Collectivisation				
3				

3. Revise actively

When faced with revising for GCSE History, most students say:

The ideas in this book are aimed at helping you to remember the core content.

Use the revision tasks in this book

The best way to remember information is to use it – to revise actively. To take an everyday example: to start with it is difficult to remember a new telephone number, but the more you use it the easier it is to remember it.

Throughout this book, you will find revision tasks. Don't miss them out. If you do the tasks you will have to use the information in the book. If you use the information you will remember it better. The more you use the information the better you will remember it.

Use the 'key words' method

Think of your brain as a computer. To read a file on a computer you need to know the name of the file. The file name is the key, and if you do not have this key you cannot get to the file, even though the computer has the file in its memory.

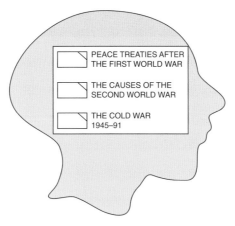

Your brain works in a similar way. When you read something it goes in, but to get the information out again you need the key to unlock your memory. So, one way to jog your memory is to use a 'key words' method. This is how it works.

1   As you read through each paragraph, highlight one or two key words. For example, when answering the question:

'What were the main political and economic features of the USA during the 1920s?'

- It had a *democratic system of government*. The President and Congress of the USA were chosen in free democratic elections.
- It had a *capitalist economy*. Business and property were privately owned. Individuals could make profits in business or move jobs if they wished. However, they might also go bankrupt or lose their jobs.
- The USA was the world's wealthiest country, but under capitalism there were always *great contrasts* – some people were very rich, others were very poor.

2   You can then use cue cards, or the key content list at the end of each chapter, to summarise your key words for each subheading. In this way you can summarise a whole topic on one sheet.

3   Later on, return to your revision plan and see whether you can recall or rewrite important paragraphs using just the key words to jog your memory.

Other revision ideas

Different people revise in different ways and you may have your own ideas on how to work. Here are some other techniques that students have used.

- summarising events in diagrams or pictures
- making a recording of the text and playing it back
- using acronyms or mnemonics
- working with friends:
    - testing each other
    - comparing your answers to practice questions.

How to use this book

Each chapter follows the same format:
- The key issues are listed on the first page of each chapter.
- The content follows exactly what the Edexcel specification says within those key issues.
- Key terms are highlighted in **bold** with an explanation nearby in the margin.
- There are revision tasks that are intended to make you think about what you are revising. Sometimes there are exam tips that also aim to get you to think in terms of the requirements of a particular question.
- Sometimes there are comments in the margin providing some information of interest.

How to succeed in Edexcel Modern World History

You will be examined on three units. Here is a summary of the content and assessment for the three units you will have to study.

Unit	Content	Examination
1	Three from: ● International rivalry, 1900–14 ● The peace settlement: 1918–28 ● International relations, 1929–39 ● How did the Cold War develop? 1943–56 ● Three Cold War crises: c.1957–69 ● Why did the Cold War end? 1979–91	75 minutes *60 marks*
2	One from: ● Germany, 1918–39 ● Russia, 1917–39 ● The USA, 1919–41	75 minutes *50 marks*
3	One from: ● War and the transformation of British society c.1903–28 ● War and the transformation of British society c.1931–51 ● A divided union? The USA, 1945–70	75 minutes *50 marks*

How to succeed in Edexcel Unit I

This is the unit which examines your knowledge and understanding of international relations.

Content

You will need to revise **three** of the first six chapters:
1 Why did war break out in 1914? International rivalry, 1900–14 (pages 10–17)
2 The peace settlement: 1918–28 (pages 18–26)
3 Why did war break out in 1939? International relations, 1929–39 (pages 27–36)
4 How did the Cold War develop? 1943–56 (pages 37–46)
5 Three Cold War crises: Berlin, Cuba and Czechoslovakia c.1957–69 (pages 47–52)
6 Why did the Cold War end? The invasion of Afghanistan to the collapse of the Soviet Union, 1979–91 (pages 52–57)

Make sure that you only revise the chapters that cover what you have studied!

The examination

In the examination, there is one set of three questions on each of the six chapters. The three questions will always be of the same types (see below) and appear in the same order. Remember you will have to answer a set of three questions on each of your **three** options.

Question (a): description

> Describe **one** decision that was made about Germany at the Potsdam Conference. *(2 marks)*

- State the factor.
- Add a sentence developing that factor.

Question (b): brief description of key features

Briefly explain the key features of the Marshall Plan (1947).   *(6 marks)*

- You will need *developed* statements about **three** key features: this means giving the feature and then explaining it. Remember this can include causes, events or consequences.
- Ensure your key features are in the right sequence.
- You will get higher marks for more precise explanations.

Question (c): essay explaining causation

Explain why the peace settlement was changed in the years 1920–28.   *(12 marks)*

- Underline key points in the question.
- Plan your answer and remember to include an introduction and a conclusion.
- Ensure that you focus on reasons for change.
- You need at least **three** reasons.
- Fully develop each reason you give.
- Make links between one reason and the next. Use link words or phrases such as 'furthermore', 'moreover', 'however', 'in addition', 'as a result of' and 'this led to'.
- Make a judgement on the importance of each reason. Try to prioritise their importance.
- Make a final judgement giving what you think is the most important or fundamental reason.

Make a copy of the following table and use it to plan causation questions.

	Explanation
Introduction	
First reason	
Link	
Second reason	
Link	
Third reason	
Link	
Conclusion	

How to succeed in Edexcel Unit 2

This is the unit which examines your knowledge and understanding of **one** of the depth studies.

Content

You will need to revise **one** of the following chapters:

7 Germany, 1918–39 (pages 58–71)
8 Russia, 1917–39 (pages 72–84)
9 The USA, 1919–41 (pages 85–96)

Make sure that you only revise the chapter that covers what you have studied!

The examination

In this examination you will answer six questions.

Question 1(a): an inference question

What can you learn from Source A about Nazi attitudes towards the churches in Germany?   *(4 marks)*

This question is asking you to read between the lines of the source and to get a message from the source.
- Make at least **one** inference.
- Begin your answer with 'This source suggests …'. This should help you focus on the question.
- Support your inference by reference to the source. In other words, use a quotation from the source.

Question 1(b): a brief description

Describe the measures taken in the Treaty of Versailles to limit German power.   *(6 marks)*

This is asking you to describe at least **two** factors.
- Give the factors.
- Describe the factors.
- Remember to focus on key words in the question.

Questions 1(c) and 1(d): causation and consequence

Explain the effects of the Reichstag fire in 1933.   *(8 marks)*

Explain why Hitler carried out a policy of persecution of the Jews and other minority groups in the years 1933–39.   *(8 marks)*

- Underline key points in the question.
- Ensure that you focus on causes/consequences. Begin each paragraph by stating the cause and then fully develop each cause you give. Use precise knowledge which will impress the examiner.
- Aim to write about at least two causes/consequences.
- Make links between one cause and the next. Use link words or phrases such as 'furthermore', 'moreover', 'however', 'in addition', 'as a result of', and 'this led to'.
- In your conclusion prioritise the importance of the causes or consequences. In other words decide which was the most important and explain why.

Question 2(a) or 2(b): change

(a) Explain how Germany recovered from its economic and political difficulties in the years 1924–29 under Stresemann's leadership.   *(8 marks)*

Or

(b) Explain how the position of young people changed in Germany in the years 1933–39.   *(8 marks)*

- Highlight key words, events, dates, etc. in the question.
- You will need to explain a minimum of two changes.
- Aim to write two paragraphs.
- At the beginning of each paragraph focus on the idea of change, e.g. 'The first change was …'.
- Make a link with the next change.
- Write a conclusion in which you prioritise the changes, e.g. which change do you think was the most important and why OR overall how much change was there?

Planning grid for causes, consequence and change questions:

First factor/change	<ul><li>Introduce the factor/change</li><li>Fully explain it</li><li>Make a judgement on its importance</li><li>Make a link with the next factor/change</li></ul> *Use link words or phrases such as 'moreover', 'however', 'therefore', 'as a result of', 'this led to', 'consequently'*
Second factor/change	<ul><li>Introduce the factor/change</li><li>Fully explain it</li><li>Make a judgement on its importance</li></ul>
Conclusion	<ul><li>Begin with 'Overall'</li><li>Again link the two factors/changes</li><li>Prioritise – put the factors/changes in order of importance and explain your decision</li></ul>

Question 3: scaffolding question

You will be given a choice of two questions, each of which will have four points (known as scaffolding) to help you answer the question.

> (a) Was the effect of reparations the main reason why the Weimar Republic found it difficult to govern Germany in the years 1919–24? Explain your answer.
> You may use the following information to help you with your answer:
> - the effects of reparations
> - attacks on the Government by left- and right-wing political parties
> - the French occupation of the Ruhr
> - the weaknesses of the Constitution
>
> *(16 marks)*

- Ensure that you do not simply describe the four parts of the scaffolding.
- Focus on the key words in the question.
- Make use of each part of the scaffolding. The examiner will often have put the points in a logical or chronological order.
- Remember to make a judgement about the important of each factor and then an overall judgement at the end.
- Do a quick plan making use of each part of the scaffolding.
- Write a conclusion which gives your overall judgement on the question. Remember, you need to make a decision on the relative importance of all four factors. You could decide that all four were equally important or some were more important than others. Give a reason for your judgement.

Planning grid for scaffolding questions:

First paragraph	• Introduce the first factor which should be the factor mentioned in the actual question • Fully explain the first factor • Make a judgement on the importance of that factor • Make a link to the second factor
Second paragraph	• Introduce the second factor • Fully explain the second factor • Make a judgement on the importance of that factor • Make a link to the third factor
Third paragraph	• Introduce the third factor • Fully explain the third factor • Make a judgement on the importance of that factor • Make a link to the fourth factor
Fourth paragraph	• Introduce the fourth factor • Fully explain the fourth factor • Make a judgement on the importance of that factor • Make a link to the additional factor
Conclusion	• Begin with 'Overall' • Make a final judgement on the relative importance of all four factors

How to succeed in Edexcel Unit 3

This is the unit which examines your source skills as well as your knowledge and understanding.

Content

You will need to revise **one** of the following three chapters:
10 War and the transformation of British society *c.*1903–28 (pages 97–112)
11 War and the transformation of British society *c.*1931–51 (pages 113–28)
12 A divided union? The USA, 1945–70 (pages 129–40)
Make sure that you only revise the chapters that cover what you have studied!

The examination

In the examination, you have to answer **five** source questions.

Question 1: inference

> What can you learn from Source A about events at Little Rock High School in 1957? *(6 marks)*

This question is asking you to read between the lines of the source and to get a message from it.

- Make at least **two** inferences.
- Begin your answer with 'This source suggests …'. This should help you focus on the question.
- Support each inference by reference to the source. In other words, quote from the source each time.

Question 2: source analysis

> Study Source C. Why was the photograph published so widely in the USA? Use details from the source and your own knowledge to explain your answer. *(8 marks)*

- Begin by explaining what the source is suggesting.
- Explain the message of the source using examples from the source.
- Fully explain the purpose of the source. In other words, what it is trying to make people think or do. Support this with evidence from the source.
- Support the purpose of the source with your own contextual knowledge. In other words, what else you know about the event.

Question 3: cross referencing

> How far do Sources A and B agree with Source C about the events at Little Rock High School? Explain your answer. *(10 marks)*

- You need to compare the three sources for support and challenge in terms of content and reliability/typicality.
- You need to make judgements on the extent of support between the sources in content and typicality/reliability.

Planning grid for cross-referencing questions:

Sources A and C	Support	Challenge
Content		
Reliability/typicality		
Sources B and C	**Support**	**Challenge**
Content		
Reliability/typicality		

	Strong support	Some support	Little support	No support
Sources A and C				
Sources B and C				

Question 4: utility questions

> How useful are Sources D and E as evidence of the Montgomery Bus Boycott? Explain your answer. *(10 marks)*

This table will help you to plan your explanation of the usefulness and limitations of each source.

	Usefulness	Limitations
Content	The source is useful because of what it tells you about the event or person. It contains facts such as …	• It only provides a limited view of the event. It does not tell us … • It is not accurate because … • It is mainly opinions, such as …, rather than facts.
Nature	The source is useful because it is a newspaper, poster, photograph or …	• The photograph only gives one limited view of the event. • The poster/newspaper exaggerates the event.
Who wrote it	It was written by someone whose views are worth knowing. Why?	The author is very one-sided and/or did not witness the event.
When was it written	• It was written at the time by an eyewitness. It gives the feelings/views of that time. • It was written later and the writer had the benefit of hindsight.	• It was written at the time and so does not have the benefit of hindsight. • It was written later and the author has forgotten important events …
Purpose	It reflects the purpose of the author, e.g. propaganda.	It does not give a balanced view because its purpose is to win the support of the reader for …

Question 5: hypothesis question

'The Montgomery Bus Boycott was the main reason for progress in civil rights for African Americans in the years 1945–60'. How far do the sources in this Unit support this statement?
Use details from the sources and your own knowledge to explain your answer. *(16 marks)*

- Decide which sources:
  - agree with the view
  - disagree with the view.
  Remember that some sources might be used to agree *and* disagree with the view.
- Make a judgement on the reliability of each source in supporting or disagreeing with the view. You will bring in your own contextual knowledge to make this judgement.

Planning grid for hypothesis questions:

Source	Agrees with interpretation	Disagrees with interpretation	Reliable	Unreliable
A				
B				
C				
D				
E				
F				

Online resources

This revision guide is also supported by online exam practice *Practise Every Question in Edexcel GCSE Modern World History*. It provides hours of exam practice for whole class teaching. With specification matching questions and sample answers, alongside an advanced and intuitive search facility, it will help you to develop your confidence and improve your grades.

The period 1900–14 saw rivalry between the Great Powers of Europe, with crises in Morocco and Bosnia bringing war closer. The assassination of the Austrian Archduke Franz Ferdinand in July 1914 set off a chain of events that led to the outbreak of the First World War.

Key issues

As with all examination topics, you will be expected to do more than simply learn the content and write it out again. You will need to show understanding of key issues from the period. These are:

- the alliance system and international rivalry between the Great Powers, 1900–14
- the growth of tension in Europe, 1900–14
- the struggle for control in the Balkans, 1900–14.

1.1 The alliance system and international rivalry between the Great Powers, 1900–14

In 1900 Europe contained the most powerful countries in the world and was dominated by six 'Great Powers': Britain, France, Germany, Austria–Hungary, Russia and Italy. Each of these powers wanted to control as much of the world's trade, and therefore become as wealthy as possible. This meant they were rivals.

The alliance system before 1914

By 1907 Europe was divided into two rival groups. These were the Triple Alliance of Germany, Austria–Hungary and Italy, and the Triple Entente of Britain, France and Russia.

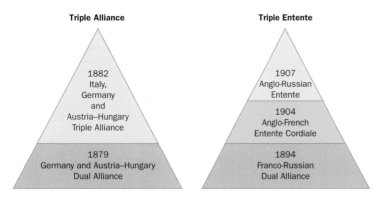

The formation of the Triple Alliance and the Triple Entente.

Exam tip Be aware of what was agreed in this alliance. This detail will impress an examiner.

The Triple Alliance

In 1879 the German **Chancellor** Bismarck signed the Dual Alliance with Austria to strengthen Germany against France and Russia. Three years later Italy joined and it became the Triple Alliance in 1882.

Key terms

Chancellor: chief minister (equivalent of Prime Minister in Britain).

The Triple Entente

This came together in three different stages:

1. The Franco-Russian Dual Alliance of 1894

These two countries allied for the following reasons:
- Kaiser Wilhelm II did not favour close relations with Russia.
- Both countries felt isolated in Europe.

2. The Entente Cordiale of 1904

At the end of the nineteenth century, Great Britain played very little part in events in Europe. This isolation, because it was a deliberate policy by Britain, became known as 'splendid isolation'. However, in 1904 France and Britain, who had been great rivals for many years, surprisingly signed an **entente** which became known as the Entente Cordiale. This was a result of two factors:
- Britain felt increasingly isolated, especially as Germany had declined to sign an agreement in the years 1900–02 limiting naval expansion.
- France continued to want revenge on Germany and the recovery of the lost provinces.

As a result of the Entente Cordiale, France allowed Britain to go ahead with reforms in Egypt and Britain promised not to oppose any French action in Morocco. Although only a loose agreement, it had some important effects:
- Kaiser Wilhelm was suspicious of the agreement and became determined to break it up.
- It encouraged French expansion into Morocco.
- Anglo-French relations drew closer in the years after 1904 so that by 1914 the two countries even planned how to fight a future war against Germany.

3. The Anglo-Russian Agreement of 1907

This was signed mainly due to French influence as France was already in alliance with Russia and had signed the Entente Cordiale. Britain now had agreements with both France and Russia and this is often referred to as the Triple Entente, although no such alliance actually existed.

The importance of the alliance system

The alliance system, including the Triple Alliance and the Triple Entente, was important because:
- it increased tension in Europe, like two rival gangs fighting for influence
- a dispute between one of the members could well involve the other members. This would turn a dispute between two countries into a major conflict between all six Great Powers.

> **Key terms**
>
> **Entente:** not an alliance, but an agreement to settle differences.

Revision tasks

1 Make a copy of the following table and complete each section.

Alliance/agreement	Members	Why signed	What agreed
Triple Alliance			
Entente Cordiale			
Anglo-Russian Entente			

2 In five words or fewer, summarise the importance of the alliance system.

3 Explain why Europe was divided into two armed camps by 1907.

> **Exam tip: q3** This is a Unit 1 style question. You will need to:
> - identify at least three reasons
> - make links between each of these reasons
> - prioritise the reasons. In other words explain which you think was the most important and why.

1.2 The growth of tension in Europe, 1900–14

In the years 1900–14 there was increasing rivalry and tension between the Great Powers due to the arms race and economic and colonial rivalry.

The arms race

In the years before 1914 there was competition between the Great Powers in the size and strength of their armed forces, including their armies and navies.

Military

Every major power in Europe, except Britain, had introduced **conscription** which led to huge armies. These armies could be mobilised at a moment's notice. From 1900–14, the main European powers more than doubled their spending on their armies. Guns, shells and bullets were stockpiled in case of war. More destructive weapons were developed like the machine gun and huge field guns.

Naval

Another aspect of the arms race was the naval competition between Britain and Germany. The navy was vital to Britain in order to protect its empire, prevent invasion and guarantee its position as a great power. Germany already had the world's best army. However, in 1898, Germany began to build a fleet of battleships to rival the British navy.

At first this was not a major threat to Britain because the Royal Navy was far superior and it would take Germany many years to catch up. However, this all changed with the launch of the British super-battleship HMS *Dreadnought* in 1906. *Dreadnought* was faster, bigger and had a much greater firing range than existing battleships. It made all previous battleships **obsolete.** Germany responded by building its own Dreadnought battleships.

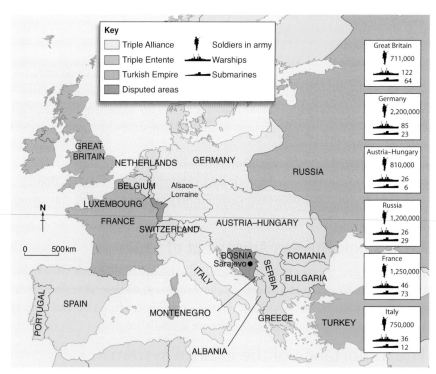

The military capacity of Europe's alliances, 1914.

This meant that everything now depended on the Dreadnought. A race developed between the two countries to see who could build the most. In 1909, Britain had eight Dreadnoughts to Germany's seven.

1906		
1907		
1908		
1909		
1910		
1911		
1912		
1913		
1914		

Britain	Total built by 1914: 29	Germany	Total built by 1914: 17

Number of Dreadnoughts built by Britain and Germany, 1906–14.

The naval race poisoned relations between Britain and Germany. Britain feared German world domination if the Kaiser had both the strongest army and navy.

It can also be argued that the arms race made war more likely:

- It increased tension between the Great Powers because as one power increased its army, another would follow suit to match it.
- As each country increased its army and weapons it became even more confident of success in a future war and more willing to test its armed forces.

> ### Revision tasks
>
> 1 Write your own definitions of the following terms:
>   - conscription   - Dreadnought   - naval race
>
> 2 Briefly explain the key features of the Anglo-German naval arms race.

Comment

Some historians believe that the arms race made war less likely. They argue that the build-up of armies, navies and weapons acted as a deterrent in a similar way to the nuclear arms race that followed the Second World War.

Exam tip: q2 This is a Unit 1 question. You will need to give at least three precise developed statements to achieve full marks.

Economic rivalry

At the beginning of the twentieth century, Britain had been the most powerful country in the world, with the largest empire and the richest trade. However, by 1914 Germany had overtaken Britain. It produced more iron, more steel and more cars.

Colonial rivalry

Another reason for tension between the Great Powers was ownership of overseas lands – colonies. In 1914 many people lived in colonies owned by the Great Powers. Colonies were important because:

- they provided cheap raw materials for industry in Europe
- they were places where the Europeans could sell their home-produced goods
- they were important trading or military bases. For example, Britain controlled the Suez Canal in Egypt, a shortcut from the Mediterranean to the Red Sea which made British possessions in India and the Far East more accessible.

Wilhelm became Kaiser (Emperor) of Germany in 1888. He wanted Germany to also have what he called 'a place in the sun'. However, any colonies Germany gained would be at the expense of Britain and France. This rivalry increased during the Moroccan crises.

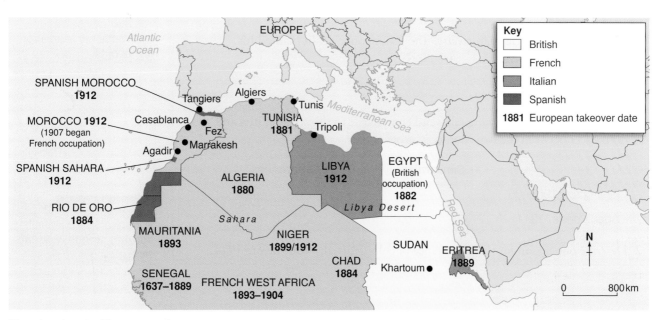

Map showing the Moroccan crises.

The first Moroccan crisis, 1905–06

France already had an empire in North Africa, which included Algeria and Tunisia. Morocco would complete this North African Empire. The Kaiser, however, decided to interfere in Morocco.

- Wilhelm wanted to test the strength of the Entente Cordiale and hoped to split it apart. He did not believe Britain would stand by France over Morocco.
- He did not want to see France extend her North African Empire.

In 1905, the Kaiser paid a visit to the Moroccan port of Tangiers where he made a speech declaring that Morocco should remain independent of France. This sparked off a crisis. France, supported by Britain, refused to back down. However, the French did agree to the Kaiser's demand for an international conference to discuss the future of Morocco.

The conference took place at Algeciras in Spain in 1906 and was a disaster for the Kaiser. Only Austria–Hungary supported his demands for Moroccan independence. Britain fully supported the French. The crisis had important effects on the alliances:

- France was given a free hand in Morocco and was grateful to the British.
- The Kaiser's attempts to break up the Entente Cordiale had backfired. His interference had strengthened relations between Britain and France.
- Anglo-German rivalry intensified as the Kaiser blamed the British for his humiliating defeat.

The second Moroccan, or Agadir, crisis, 1911

In 1911, the French finally occupied Fez in Morocco. The Kaiser sent a gunboat called the *Panther* to the Moroccan port of Agadir in order to force the French to agree to compensation in the form of the French Congo in central Africa.

However, Germany's actions backfired. Britain was determined to support France as they both believed that Wilhelm was trying to set up a German naval base in Morocco. Lloyd George, the British Chancellor of the Exchequer and a well known pacifist, made a speech in the Mansion House in London in which he directly warned the Germans that Britain would back the French, by war if necessary. Britain's fleet was even prepared for war. In the end Germany backed down rather than risk war.

The crisis had some important effects:

- It greatly increased tension in Europe.
- It strengthened the Anglo-French Entente due to British support for the French.
- The Kaiser suffered another humiliating defeat and was unlikely to back down a third time.
- It increased Anglo-German rivalry. The Kaiser once again blamed his humiliation on the British.

Exam tip Candidates often confuse the key features of these two Moroccan crises. Ensure you revise them thoroughly. You may well be asked to explain the key features of one or both.

Revision tasks

1 Make a copy of the following table and complete it to show similarities and differences between the two Moroccan crises.

	Similarities	Differences
First crisis, 1905–06		
Agadir crisis, 1911		

2 Describe one reason for the importance of colonies in the years before 1914.

Exam tip: q2 This is a Unit 1 style question. You only need to write two sentences.

1.3 The struggle for control in the Balkans, 1900–14

The main trouble spot was the area of south-east Europe known as the Balkans. This area had been part of the Ottoman (Turkish) Empire since the seventeenth century. However, the Ottoman Empire declined in the nineteenth century with countries such as Greece, Bulgaria and Serbia achieving their independence.

Rivalry of the Great Powers

These changes encouraged the intervention of the Great Powers who all had different interests in the area.

Austria–Hungary

Austria–Hungary felt increasingly threatened by Serbian nationalism in the years after 1900. The main concern of the Austro-Hungarian Government was that the population of Serbs within its empire would want to be part of a greater Serbia, which might in turn lead to a break-up of the Austro-Hungarian Empire. Austria–Hungary, fully supported by Germany, became determined to crush Serbia especially when it was greatly strengthened by the Balkan Wars of 1912–13.

Serbia

Serbia wished to unite all Serbs living in south-east Europe in an enlarged state of Greater Serbia and was supported by Russia who regarded herself as the protector of all **Slavs**.

Russia

The Russians were also Slavs and were keen to promote Slav nationalism and thus help the Slav people in the region to win their freedom from the Ottomans. In addition they supported greater Serbian nationalism, believing this would break up the empire of their biggest rival, Austria–Hungary.

> **Key terms**
>
> **Slavs:** the name given to the different national groups who live in the Balkans, the area of south-eastern Europe.

The Balkan crises, 1908–13

This rivalry led to two serious crises in the years before 1914.

The Bosnian crisis, 1908–09

The Balkans in 1908 (shown by the area in red).

> **Comment**
>
> *The Bosnian crisis of 1908–09 is often described as a dress rehearsal for the crisis that followed the assassination at Sarajevo in 1914.*

In 1908, Austria–Hungary **annexed** Bosnia and Herzegovina.

This led to a serious international crisis. The Serbs were furious because they had hoped to make Bosnia part of a greater Serbian state. They appealed to Russia for help. Russia's answer was to call for an international conference to discuss the annexation. Austria–Hungary refused to attend and was fully backed by Germany.

Germany demanded that Russia accept the annexation. Russia had little choice but to back down as its army was no match for the German forces. This crisis again increased tension between the Great Powers:

- Russia was humiliated and so was unlikely to back down in another crisis.
- Germany was now fully committed to supporting Austro-Hungarian policy in the Balkans, even if it led to war.
- Russia drew even closer to Britain and France.

The Balkan Wars, 1912–13

In 1912 Serbia, Greece, Bulgaria and Montenegro formed the Balkan League and attacked the Turks in order to finally drive them out of the Balkans. In just three weeks the Turks were driven back to Adrianople and almost out of Europe. The Great Powers met in London and drew up a treaty which ended the first Balkan war.

However, within a month Bulgaria, unhappy with its gains in the Treaty of London, attacked its former allies, particularly the Serbs. The Serbs, supported by the Turks and Romania, defeated the Bulgars. As a result of these wars:

- rivalry between Austria–Hungary and Serbia was increased. Serbia had nearly doubled in size and now posed a much greater threat. Austria–Hungary was more determined than ever to crush the Serbs
- during the wars the Serbs had gained part of the Adriatic coast and, for the first time, access to the sea. However, at Austria–Hungary's insistence this land was taken away from the Serbs, who were furious.

Revision tasks

1 Why did the Bosnian crisis increase rivalry between:
   - Austria–Hungary and Serbia
   - Austria–Hungary and Russia
   - Russia and Germany?

2 Why was the crisis settled without resorting to war?

3 Draw a mind map showing the key features of the Balkan Wars, 1912–13.

4 Explain why events in the Balkans, 1908–13, increased rivalry between the Great Powers.

Sarajevo and its consequences

The immediate reason for the outbreak of war was the assassination of Archduke Franz Ferdinand in Sarajevo in June 1914.

The assassination

On 28 June 1914 Archduke Franz Ferdinand and his wife, Sophie, were assassinated by Gavrilo Princip, a member of the 'Black Hand' terrorist organisation, during a state visit to Sarajevo. Austria–Hungary was furious and blamed the Serbs. Having secured full backing from the Kaiser, on 23 July Austria–Hungary sent an **ultimatum** to Serbia which it knew the Serbs would reject.

The ultimatum included ten demands that meant the virtual end of Serbian independence. Surprisingly, the Serbs accepted all but one. However, Austria–Hungary, determined on revenge, declared war on Serbia on 28 July 1914.

Key terms

Annexed: to seize territory and make part of an empire.
Ultimatum: a final demand – or else!

Comment

In 1911 the Black Hand terrorist group formed, which aimed to unite all Serbs into a greater Serbia. By 1914 it had 2,500 members. It planned to assassinate Archduke Franz Ferdinand, the heir to the throne of Austria–Hungary, when he visited Sarajevo in June 1914.

Exam tip Questions on the Balkan Wars are confusing and often not well answered. Ensure you revise this section thoroughly. The easiest way to remember is:
- in the first war the Balkan states fought against Turkey
- in the second war the Balkan states fought against Bulgaria.

Exam tip: q4 This is a Unit 1 style question. You will need to:
- identify at least three reasons
- make links between each of these reasons
- prioritise the reasons. In other words, explain which you think was the most important and why.

The events leading to the outbreak of war

Each country had to **mobilise** quickly to gain an advantage. Once one country began to move its troops to the front line, the enemy had to do the same or risk immediate defeat. In other words, once mobilisation began it was difficult to stop. Here are the events which led to the outbreak of the First World War.

28 July		Austria declares war on Serbia.
30 July		Russia starts moving its armed forces to help Serbia defend itself against Austria–Hungary. Germany warns Russia to stop mobilising. Russia ignores the warning.
1 August		Germany declares war on Russia and warns France to remain neutral. Italy declares that it will remain neutral.
2 August		France begins to mobilise its armed forces.
3 August		Germany declares war on France.
4 August		Germany invades Belgium as part of the Schlieffen Plan. Later that day, Britain declares war on Germany.

The Austro-Hungarian declaration of war on Serbia triggered the alliance system and turned a local war between two countries into a general European war.

- German backing encouraged Austria–Hungary to declare war on Serbia.
- Russia, the protector of Serbia, was not prepared to back down, unlike in 1908–09.
- France, an ally of Russia, refused Germany's demands to remain neutral.
- Britain declared war on Germany because of the German invasion of Belgium, and its closer relations with France following the signing of the Entente Cordiale.

Comment

It has been suggested that Austria–Hungary deliberately set up the assassination of the Archduke to provide an excuse to crush Serbia. After all, the Archduke travelled in an open-top car and the visit coincided with Serbian National Day.

Revision tasks

1 Draw a timeline to show the main developments of 1900–14. Indicate on your timeline how these developments increased rivalry between the Great Powers.

2 On a sheet of A3 paper summarise the main reasons for increased rivalry and the outbreak of war in 1914.
   a) Put the reasons in order, clockwise, beginning with the most important at twelve o'clock.
   b) Draw lines to show links between the reasons. Explain the links along these lines.

3 Briefly explain the key features of the Sarajevo crisis of June–July 1914.

Exam tip Ensure you know the key dates from 28 June to 4 August 1914. Precise knowledge of dates will impress an examiner.

Key content

You need to have a good working knowledge of the following areas:

- the alliance system before 1914, including the Triple Alliance and the Triple Entente
- the arms race
- economic and colonial rivalry
- the two Moroccan crises
- Great Power rivalry in the Balkans
- the Bosnian crisis of 1908–09
- the Balkan Wars, 1912–13
- the assassination at Sarajevo and the events leading to the outbreak of war.

Exam tip: q3 This is a Unit 1 question. You will need to give at least three precise developed statements to achieve full marks.

Chapter 2: The peace settlement: 1918–28

The First World War was a disaster for Europe. Millions were killed and whole countries were devastated. The victorious leaders met in Paris in 1918 to try to work out how to stop a terrible war like this ever happening again.

Key issues

As with all examination topics, you will be expected to do more than simply learn the content and write it out again. You will need to show understanding of key issues from this period. These are:

- the Paris Peace Conference and the 'Big Three'
- the peace treaties and the impact on the defeated powers
- the creation and peacekeeping role of the League of Nations in the 1920s and the work of its agencies.

2.1 The Paris Peace Conference and the aims of the 'Big Three'

In November 1918 Germany signed the armistice which ended the First World War. This was followed by the Paris Peace Conference which was dominated by the 'Big Three': the leaders of Britain, the USA and France.

The armistice

Germany agreed to an **armistice** on 11 November 1918 because revolution in Germany in early November had led to the abdication of Kaiser Wilhelm II and the setting up of a new German republic. The new republic realised the German army had been defeated. The armistice terms demanded that Germany:

- withdraw all its troops from occupied countries in the west and give up any land it had won in the east against Russia
- withdraw its troops 30 miles from the east bank of the Rhine, with the Allied troops on the west side ready to cross this land if the armistice broke down
- surrender huge numbers of artillery, machine guns, aircraft and its submarine fleet
- allow its navy to be moved to Allied ports and placed under Allied control.

The 'Big Three'

The most important and influential countries at the Paris peace negotiations were France, Britain and the USA. Their leaders became known as the 'Big Three' and had conflicting views of the aims of the peace treaty.

Leader	Views on peace treaty
 Georges Clemenceau of France	During the war, France had suffered enormous damage with large areas of land devastated, many factories destroyed and over a million deaths. Clemenceau was under pressure from the French people to make Germany suffer. He also wanted to prevent future threats of a German invasion. Therefore he wanted a harsh treaty which would punish Germany and cripple its economy so it could not threaten France again.
 Woodrow Wilson of the USA	The USA had only been in the war since April 1917. Its war damage and casualties were low compared to France and Britain. Wilson's ideas were very much influenced by his Fourteen Points (see below). Although he believed that Germany was responsible for the war, he did not want to impose a harsh treaty as this would lead to a German desire for revenge and another war. Wilson had two main aims: ● **self-determination** ● international co-operation: settling disputes by all countries working together.
 David Lloyd George of Great Britain	The British people were bitter towards Germany. They wanted a harsh peace treaty and Lloyd George had promised that he would make Germany pay. However, like Wilson, he feared that a harsh treaty might lead to a German desire for revenge and possibly another war. He also wanted Britain and Germany to begin trading with each other again. Lloyd George was often in the middle ground between Clemenceau, who he thought was too extreme, and Wilson, who he believed was too reliant on the Fourteen Points.

Exam tip You need to remember not only the views of the Big Three but also how these would lead to clashes and differences.

Key terms

Self-determination: the right of nations to rule themselves.

The Fourteen Points

In January 1918, President Wilson of the USA had proposed the Fourteen Points which he said should be the key to a fair peace. His ideas included:

● a ban on secret treaties and a reduction in arms
● the idea that countries should not claim colonies without consulting each other and the local inhabitants
● self-determination for countries which were once part of the Turkish and Austro-Hungarian Empires.

Exam tip You do not need to know all Fourteen Points, only the main ideas which are summarised here.

Revision tasks

1 What is meant by:
● an armistice
● the Fourteen Points
● self-determination?

2 Make a copy of the triangle (right). On one side of each line write in green any similarities in the aims of each leader. On the other side write in red any differences.

```
        Clemenceau

   Wilson    Lloyd George
```

3 Where would you put each leader on this line?

Moderate treaty ⟵————————⟶ Harsh treaty

4 Describe one reason why the Big Three disagreed.

Exam tip: q4 This is the style of the first question on Unit 1. It is worth two marks and requires only two sentences.

2.2 The peace treaties and the impact on the defeated powers

Twenty-seven nations were represented at the Paris Peace Conference but the defeated countries were not allowed to attend. Each defeated country had to sign a separate treaty with the victorious **Allies.**

The Treaty of Versailles

This was the treaty imposed on Germany, whose leaders were told the terms in May 1919 and forced to sign in the following month. The main terms were as follows:

War guilt

Article 231, the 'war guilt' clause: Germany had to agree that it was responsible for starting the war.

German armed forces

- The army was limited to 100,000.
- Conscription was banned. Soldiers had to be volunteers.
- Germany was not allowed armoured vehicles, submarines or military aircraft.
- The navy could have only six battleships and 30 smaller ships.
- The Rhineland, the area between Germany and France, became a **demilitarised** zone. The Allies were to keep an army of occupation on the west bank of the Rhine for fifteen years. No German troops were allowed into that area.

Reparations

The Allies agreed that Germany should pay compensation to France, Britain and Belgium for the damage caused by the war. These payments were known as **reparations**. The exact figure of £6,600 million was set by a reparations commission in 1921.

Loss of territories

The Allies agreed that lands and territories would be rearranged.

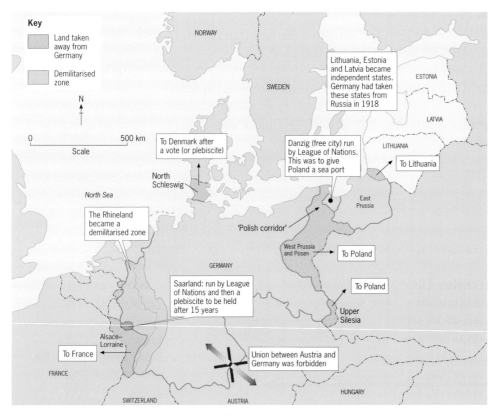

German territories lost after the Treaty of Versailles.

Key terms

Allies: countries fighting on the same side against Germany.
Demilitarised: no armed forces or weapons.
Reparations: repair, or compensation for damage caused.

Comment

Demilitarisation, and the other military terms of the treaty, were influenced by Clemenceau to safeguard France against another German invasion.

Comment

The terms of the reparations were influenced by Clemenceau who wanted to cripple the German economy.

The territorial terms were partly influenced by Clemenceau, with the return of Alsace–Lorraine, but also Wilson and the goal of self-determination in eastern Europe.

In addition German colonies, mainly in Africa, were given to France and Britain under the control of the League of Nations.

Anschluss

This means the joining together of Austria and Germany and was forbidden by the Treaty of Versailles.

The League of Nations

Previous methods of keeping the peace had failed and so the League of Nations was set up as an international 'police force' (see pages 23–5). Germany was not invited to join the League until it had proved that it had become a peace-loving country.

> **Exam tip** Candidates are frequently asked questions about the terms of the Treaty of Versailles. The more precise and detailed your knowledge, the higher your marks.

German reactions to the Treaty of Versailles

The Germans reacted to the Treaty with horror and outrage.

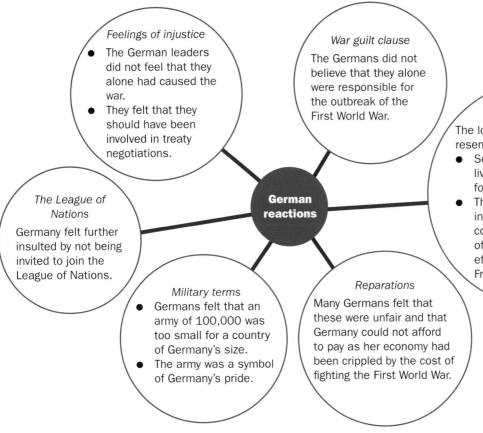

Feelings of injustice
- The German leaders did not feel that they alone had caused the war.
- They felt that they should have been involved in treaty negotiations.

War guilt clause
The Germans did not believe that they alone were responsible for the outbreak of the First World War.

Loss of territory
The loss of territory was deeply resented by the German people.
- Some Germans were now living in countries ruled by foreign governments.
- The Saar, an important industrial area, was now controlled by the League of Nations but had been effectively taken over by France.

The League of Nations
Germany felt further insulted by not being invited to join the League of Nations.

German reactions

Military terms
- Germans felt that an army of 100,000 was too small for a country of Germany's size.
- The army was a symbol of Germany's pride.

Reparations
Many Germans felt that these were unfair and that Germany could not afford to pay as her economy had been crippled by the cost of fighting the First World War.

> ## Comment
>
> *Be aware that Germany had imposed an even harsher treaty, the Treaty of Brest-Litovsk, on Russia in March 1918. Under that treaty Russia lost nearly one-third of its land area.*

Revision tasks

1 Make a copy of the following table. For each term create a German newspaper headline summarising German reactions. One example has been done for you.

	German newspaper headline
Military terms	
Territorial losses	Germany split in two by loss of East Prussia to Poland
War guilt	
Reparations	
Anschluss	

2 In your view which of the Big Three would have been most satisfied with the Treaty of Versailles?

3 Briefly explain how the military terms affected Germany.

> **Exam tip: q3** This is the style of the second question on Unit 1. You will need to explain the terms themselves and how they would have weakened Germany.

The other peace treaties

Treaty	Country affected	Key terms
St Germain, September 1919	Austria	<ul><li>Austria agreed to the break-up of the Austro-Hungarian Empire.</li><li>It accepted Hungary, Poland, Czechoslovakia and Yugoslavia as independent countries.</li><li>Land was lost to Italy.</li><li>The army was limited to 30,000 men and it had to pay reparations.</li></ul>
Neuilly, November 1919	Bulgaria	<ul><li>Bulgaria lost land to Yugoslavia and Greece but gained land from Turkey.</li><li>It had to pay $400 million in reparations and its army was limited to 20,000 men.</li></ul>
Trianon, June 1920	Hungary	<ul><li>Hungary became an independent country.</li><li>Land was given to Czechoslovakia, Romania, Yugoslavia and Austria.</li><li>The army was limited to 35,000 men and it had to pay reparations.</li></ul>
Sèvres, August 1920	Turkey	<ul><li>Land was taken so Turkey's European possessions were limited to a small area around Constantinople.</li><li>The Turkish Empire was broken up. Iraq, Transjordan and Palestine became British **mandates**. Syria became a French mandate.</li><li>Arabia became independent.</li></ul>
Lausanne, 1923	Turkey	This changed the Treaty of Sèvres.<ul><li>Turkey recovered some of the land it lost in Europe.</li><li>It was given control of the Bosphorus strait and the Dardanelles strait.</li></ul>

Key terms

Mandate: a country placed in the care of another, in this case in the care of one of the victorious powers after the First World War.
Deutsche mark: the unit of German currency.

Changes to the treaties

There were a number of changes to the treaties in the years after 1919:

Reparations

The German Government was unable to make its first payments in 1922 due to internal economic problems. By 1923 the Allies had twice reduced the amount Germany had to pay.

The occupation of the Ruhr, 1923

In January 1923 France and Belgium lost patience with Germany and occupied the Ruhr industrial area of Germany to take payment in kind by running the industries themselves.
- The German workers refused to co-operate and went on strike.
- The German Government printed more money to pay the strikers, which led to hyperinflation. The **Deutsche Mark** lost all value.
- Relations became strained between France and Britain as the British were more sympathetic to the Germans and were against the Ruhr occupation.

The Dawes Plan, 1924

In 1924, following his brief period as German Chancellor, Gustav Stresemann was made responsible for German foreign affairs. He persuaded the USA to set up the Dawes Plan which fixed the German reparations payments on a sliding scale according to their capacity to pay. The French and Belgians agreed to withdraw their troops from the Ruhr.

The Locarno Agreements, 1925

This was a collection of seven treaties between Britain, France, Italy, Holland, Belgium, Germany, Czechoslovakia and Poland signed in Locarno, Switzerland, in October 1925. The countries agreed to respect their common borders and to go to the League of Nations if there were disputes.

Germany and the League, 1926

As a result of the Locarno Agreements Germany was admitted to the League of Nations.

The Kellogg-Briand Pact, 1928

This pact was signed by 61 countries who agreed that war was wrong and that they should always seek peaceful solutions to any problems between them.

Revision tasks

1 Which countries were forced to sign the following peace treaties?
  ● Versailles
  ● Neuilly
  ● Trianon
  ● St Germain
  ● Sèvres

2 Make a copy of the following table and complete it to show similarities and differences between the terms of the treaties imposed on the defeated nations.

Treaty	Similarities	Differences
Neuilly		
Trianon		
St Germain		
Sèvres		

3 Draw a timeline for 1920–28. On your timeline plot the changes to the peace treaties.

4 Describe one decision made at the Treaty of St Germain.

5 Briefly explain how the peace settlement changed in the 1920s.

2.3 The creation and peacekeeping role of the League of Nations in the 1920s and the work of its agencies

The League of Nations was set up in 1920 with 42 original member countries. It was based on the idea of President Woodrow Wilson with the aim of avoiding future wars, and had a **Covenant** which laid out the aims of the League:
● to prevent aggression by any nation
● to encourage co-operation between nations
● to work towards international disarmament
● to improve the living and working conditions of all peoples.

The League was built upon the idea of collective security. This meant that the members of the League could prevent war by acting together to protect and defend the interests of all nations.

The organisation of the League

The Assembly

This was the debating chamber of the League and was located at the League's headquarters in Geneva, Switzerland. When the League began there were 42 members, each with a vote in the Assembly that met once a year. It had the powers to admit new members, elect permanent members to the Council and suggest changes to existing peace treaties.

The Council

This met up to three times a year and in times of emergency. It had five permanent and four temporary members.
- The five permanent members were the major powers: Britain, France, Italy, Japan and, from 1926, Germany.
- The four temporary members were elected for three years at a time.

The Permanent Court of International Justice

This court was based at the Hague in the Netherlands. It was made up of judges who represented the different legal systems of member countries. It gave decisions on disputes between two countries if asked, but had no way of enforcing its decisions.

The International Labour Organisation (ILO)

This existed to bring about the League's aim of improving working conditions around the world. Representatives of governments, workers and employers met each year to set minimum standards and persuade members to adopt them.

The Secretariat

This was the civil service that carried out the work and administration of the League. It kept records of League meetings and prepared reports for the different organisations of the League.

Commissions

These were set up to carry out specialist work. Some of them existed only for a short period of time, such as the Refugees Commission, which helped First World War refugees return to their homes. Other commissions were more permanent, such as those set up to deal with slavery and health.

Peacekeeping role

The main duty of the Council was to solve any disputes that might occur between states. It was hoped that this would be done by negotiation. If any country was considered to have started a war through an act of aggression, then such a war became the concern of all the countries in the League who would take action against the aggressor. This action was in three stages:
- **moral condemnation**, which meant that all countries would put pressure on the aggressor in order to make them feel guilty and shame them into stopping the war and accepting the League's decision
- **economic sanctions**, which meant that all countries in the League would stop trading with the aggressor
- **military force**, in which countries in the League would contribute to an armed force that would act against the aggressor.

Exam tip Candidates often score low marks on the organisation of the League because they fail to revise this section thoroughly.

Revision tasks

1 Produce a key word list of four to six words to summarise the aims of the League of Nations.

2 Give two differences between the Council and the Assembly of the League.

3 What was meant by 'collective security'?

4 Briefly explain the key features of the organisation of the League.

The role of the special commissions

These looked into a wide range of issues.

The Mandates Commission

After the First World War fourteen territories, or mandates, previously governed by the defeated nations, were placed under the control of the victorious powers.

Comment

President Wilson founded the League but many Americans did not want the USA involved because they believed their country would be dragged into more European disputes; instead they supported a policy of isolation. The League did not have the support of the richest and most powerful country in the world.

In theory the League supervised the running of these mandates to ensure that the countries that controlled the mandates did so in the interests of the people of that territory. However, the League could not force its will on the controlling countries.

The Slavery Commission

Slavery was still practised in a number of countries, particularly in Africa. The Commission was set up to abolish slavery and its greatest successes were in freeing 200,000 slaves in Sierra Leone and fighting forced labour in Ethiopia and Liberia.

The Commission for Refugees

After the First World War there were about 500,000 prisoners of war who needed to be returned to their homelands. In less than two years the Commission had ensured that almost all the prisoners were sent home.

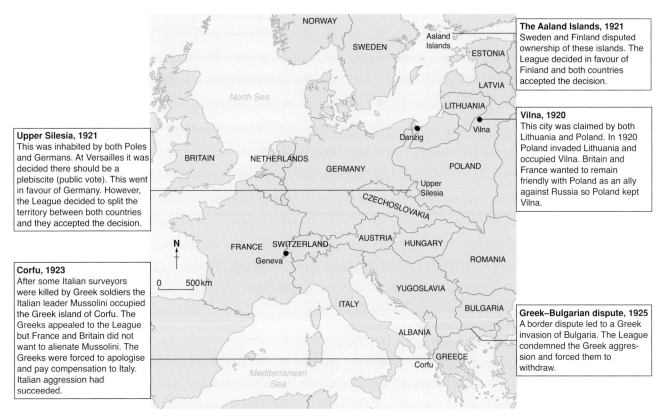

The Aaland Islands, 1921
Sweden and Finland disputed ownership of these islands. The League decided in favour of Finland and both countries accepted the decision.

Vilna, 1920
This city was claimed by both Lithuania and Poland. In 1920 Poland invaded Lithuania and occupied Vilna. Britain and France wanted to remain friendly with Poland as an ally against Russia so Poland kept Vilna.

Upper Silesia, 1921
This was inhabited by both Poles and Germans. At Versailles it was decided there should be a plebiscite (public vote). This went in favour of Germany. However, the League decided to split the territory between both countries and they accepted the decision.

Corfu, 1923
After some Italian surveyors were killed by Greek soldiers the Italian leader Mussolini occupied the Greek island of Corfu. The Greeks appealed to the League but France and Britain did not want to alienate Mussolini. The Greeks were forced to apologise and pay compensation to Italy. Italian aggression had succeeded.

Greek–Bulgarian dispute, 1925
A border dispute led to a Greek invasion of Bulgaria. The League condemned the Greek aggression and forced them to withdraw.

Successes and failures of the League in the 1920s.

The League's peacekeeping role

The League experienced successes and failure in its peacekeeping role in the 1920s.

The weaknesses of the League

- The League lacked key members from the start, including the defeated nations, Russia, and the USA.
- The League was seen as an exclusive club of victors which was very much dependent on Anglo-French co-operation. However the two countries fell out over the French occupation of the Ruhr in January 1923.
- The organisation of the League made it difficult to act quickly because one country could easily **veto** League action.
- The League lacked 'teeth'. **Economic sanctions** were often only applied in a half-hearted fashion and the League had no army.
- The world Depression brought about the rise of dictators such as Hitler who had little respect for the League.

Exam tip Candidates are often asked about the weaknesses of the League or why it failed. Remember to give several reasons, such as lack of power, weak organisation and the absence of key members.

Key terms

Economic sanctions: restrictions on trade with another country.
Veto: the right to block a decision made by others.

Revision tasks

1 Why were the following countries not members of the League in 1920?
   • Germany   • Russia   • USA

2 Describe one weakness of the League.

3 If you were the leader of a small country thinking of joining the League in 1920, what advantages and disadvantages do you think membership would give you? Complete a table like the one below.

Advantages	Disadvantages

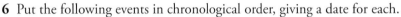

4 Make a copy of the set of scales on the right. On the left pan list the successes of the League and on the right pan list its failures. On balance, was the League a success or a failure in the 1920s?

Successes of the League   Failures of the League

5 Draw a mind map showing the main reasons for the failure of the League of Nations. On your mind map draw lines showing links between some of these reasons, then along each connecting line briefly explain the link.

6 Put the following events in chronological order, giving a date for each.
   • The Locarno Agreements   • French occupation of the Ruhr
   • Setting up of the League of Nations   • The Kellogg-Briand Pact
   • The Treaty of Versailles   • Germany joining the League of Nations.

Key content

You need to have a good working knowledge of the following areas:

- the reasons for and terms of the armistice of November 1918
- the different motives of the Big Three at Versailles
- the main terms of the Treaty of Versailles
- reasons for German opposition to the Treaty
- the main terms of the treaties of Neuilly, Trianon, St Germain, Sèvres and Lausanne
- the main post-war conferences and changes to the Versailles peace treaty, including the occupation of the Ruhr in 1923, the Locarno Agreements of 1925 and the Kellogg-Briand Pact
- the aims and organisation of the League of Nations
- the work of the League's commissions and its peacekeeping role in the 1920s
- the weaknesses of the League in the 1920s.

In 1929 the Wall Street Crash led to a serious world depression which badly affected the industrialised world. At the same time the League of Nations was unable to prevent aggression from countries such as Japan, Germany and Italy.

Key issues

As with all examination topics, you will be expected to do more than simply learn the content and write it out again. You will need to show understanding of key issues from the period. These are:

- the failure of the League of Nations: Manchuria (1931–32) and Abyssinia (1935–36)
- Hitler's challenges to the peace settlement, 1933–36
- the failure of appeasement, 1937–39.

3.1 The failure of the League of Nations: Manchuria (1931–32) and Abyssinia (1935–36)

These two major crises exposed the weaknesses of the League of Nations.

The impact of the Great Depression

In 1929 the US economy collapsed. This was due to the Wall Street Crash, when the value of shares on the New York stock market fell very quickly and the banking system subsequently collapsed. The Crash was to have dramatic effects on the USA and the world.

- American businesses experienced a huge drop in the number of goods they could sell and companies laid off workers as they cut production. By 1933 American production of manufactured goods was only 20 per cent of what it had been in 1929.
- Many European countries such as Germany were dependent on US trade and loans. Since the USA could no longer afford to import goods from overseas, the economies of these countries suffered as demand for their goods fell. The world economy went into what became known as the 'Great Depression'. This had serious effects on international relations.
- Depression and high unemployment was a major reason why Hitler came to power in Germany in January 1933.
- Much of the goodwill that had existed between nations in the 1920s collapsed.

The Manchurian crisis, 1931–33

This was the first major challenge to the League of Nations.

Causes

By the early twentieth century, Japan was a rising power in Asia and the Pacific and had developed very quickly into a modern trading nation. However, the Wall Street

Crash had a major impact on the Japanese economy. **Protectionist** policies in the USA and other countries led to a loss of trade. Japan looked for other ways to expand.

In 1931, the Japanese used the excuse of an attack by Chinese troops on a Japanese railway to invade the Chinese territory of Manchuria. Manchuria was rich in natural resources and raw materials and provided a market for Japanese goods. The invasion was a success and Manchuria was renamed Manchukuo.

<table>
<tr><td>**Key terms**</td></tr>
</table>

Key terms

Protectionist: the economic theory of using the tax system to protect home industries in the face of foreign competition.

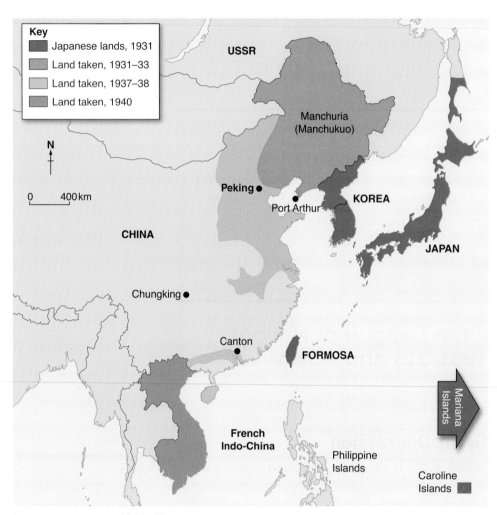

Key
- Japanese lands, 1931
- Land taken, 1931–33
- Land taken, 1937–38
- Land taken, 1940

N

0   400km

USSR

Manchuria (Manchukuo)

CHINA

Peking

Port Arthur

KOREA

JAPAN

Chungking

Canton

FORMOSA

French Indo-China

Philippine Islands

Caroline Islands

Mariana Islands

Japanese expansion, 1931–40.

Events

China was in the middle of a civil war and was unable to defend Manchuria. The Chinese appealed to the League of Nations for support against the Japanese. The League sent a commission, the Lytton Commission, to investigate the crisis. The commission was very slow and took over a year to investigate, by which time the invasion and occupation had been completed.

The League accepted the findings of the report, condemned the actions of the Japanese and asked the Japanese to withdraw from the province. The Japanese left the League and remained in control of Manchuria.

Results

This event marked the beginning of the end for the League:
- Britain and France were not willing to support the League in taking action against the Japanese.
- The League had failed to prevent aggression. This encouraged later aggression by Italy and Germany.

Comment

Britain and France both had empires in the Far East and feared possible further Japanese aggression if they fully supported the League.

Exam tip You will often be asked how and why the Manchurian crisis contributed to the failure of the League of Nations.

The Abyssinian crisis, 1935–36

This crisis greatly reduced the influence of the League.

Causes

In 1935 Italians troops invaded the African country of Abyssinia.

- Mussolini had ruled Italy since 1922 and wanted to increase Italy's prestige as a world power by increasing Italy's territories in Africa.
- Abyssinia was one of the few countries in Africa not under European control.
- The Italians wanted revenge for a humiliating defeat by the Abyssinians at the Battle of Adowa in 1896.

Events

The Emperor of Abyssinia, Haile Selassie, appealed to the League for assistance. The League condemned Italian aggression and imposed economic sanctions against Italy. However, these sanctions did not include oil and Italy continued to trade with non-League members such as the USA. France and Britain did not want to offend Mussolini and drive him closer to Hitler and Germany. The British foreign secretary even worked out a plan with the French, known as the Hoare–Laval Pact, to offer Mussolini most of Abyssinia. However, the plan had to be withdrawn when it was leaked to the public.

Italian expansion, 1934–36.

Key
- Italian advance
- Italian territory
- French territory
- British territory or strong British influence

Results

The effects of the Abyssinian crisis were serious for the League. It marked the end of the League as a peacekeeping organisation as it could no longer be taken seriously.

- The crisis showed that its members were not willing to use force to stop aggression.
- The secret deal, the Hoare–Laval Pact, had also shown Britain and France to be undermining the League.

Comment

The League remained in existence until the Second World War but became little more than a 'talking shop'.

Revision tasks

1 Make a copy of the following table and complete each box in five words or fewer.

	Causes	Events	Effects on League
Manchurian crisis			
Abyssinian crisis			

2 Which of the following were involved with the Abyssinian and Manchurian crises?
- Lytton Commission • Hoare–Laval Pact • China
- Haile Selassie • Mussolini • Economic sanctions

3 Briefly explain the key features of the Manchurian crisis, 1931–33.

Exam tip: q3 This is a Unit 1 question. You will need to give at least three precise developed statements to achieve full marks.

29

3.2 Hitler's challenges to the peace settlement, 1933–36

During this period Hitler successfully challenged the Treaty of Versailles.

Germany and the Treaty of Versailles

At the end of the First World War, Germany had expected a fair peace treaty based on Woodrow Wilson's Fourteen Points (see page 19). However, there was no negotiation and the Treaty soon became known in Germany as a *diktat* or dictated peace. Many Germans were resentful of the Treaty:

- Germany had to accept full responsibility for the war and pay heavy reparations which did much to cripple the economy and cause the hyperinflation of 1923.
- The Germans also lost a large amount of territory. Germany itself was split in two by the decision to create the 'Polish Corridor' which gave Poland access to the sea.
- There were major cutbacks in the German armed forces and no troops were allowed in the Rhineland.

Many Germans were stunned by the terms of the Treaty and blamed the new Weimar Republic for signing it. Hitler and the Nazi Party gained support from many Germans due to their promise to get rid of the Treaty of Versailles.

Hitler's aims

From January 1933 German foreign policy was controlled by Hitler.

- He took Germany out of the League of Nations which Germany had been allowed to join in 1926.
- Hitler saw the Treaty of Versailles as one of the major causes of Germany's problems. He promised the German people that he would reverse the Treaty and retake the territory that Germany had lost. He wanted to create a greater Germany or *Grossdeutschland.*
- In the longer term Hitler planned to expand into eastern Europe to give the German people *Lebensraum* which he believed they needed.

The return of the Saar

The industrial area of the Saar was taken from Germany by the Treaty of Versailles and put under the control of the League of Nations. A **plebiscite** was to be held among the population after fifteen years to decide whether it should be returned to Germany. The plebiscite was held in January 1935, when over 90 per cent voted in favour. Hitler greeted this result as a huge triumph, and declared that this was the first of the injustices of Versailles to be reversed.

Hitler and rearmament

One of Hitler's first steps on coming to power was to increase Germany's armed forces, although this had to be done secretly at first due to the terms of the Treaty of Versailles.

The Disarmament Conference, 1932–4

This Conference first met in February 1932. The Germans walked out of the Conference in July 1932 when the other powers failed to agree to disarm down to the level of Germany. In May 1933 Hitler returned to the Conference and promised not to rearm if 'in five years all other nations destroyed their arms'. When they refused Hitler withdrew from the Conference in October 1933 and, soon after, from the League of Nations.

Comment

The views of historians differ over Hitler's foreign policy. Some believe that he planned for war from the beginning. Others see Hitler as an opportunist who took chances.

Key terms

Lebensraum: living space. Hitler wanted to expand eastwards to create more space for the growing German population.
Plebiscite: a vote by the people of a state or region on an important question, such as union with another country.

Revision tasks

1 Who or what were the following:
- *Lebensraum*
- *diktat*
- *Grossdeutschland?*

2 Explain why Hitler felt so triumphant about the return of the Saar.

Non-Aggression Pact with Poland, 1934

In January 1934 Germany signed a non-aggression agreement with Poland. This was signed for several reasons:
- Hitler was hoping to weaken the existing alliance between France and Poland.
- He hoped to reduce Polish fears of German aggression.
- He wanted to show that he had no quarrel with Poland, only with the Soviet Union.

Conscription

In 1935 Hitler re-introduced conscription and announced a peacetime army of 550,000. He was breaking the terms of the Treaty of Versailles.

Representatives from France, Italy and Britain met in a town called Stresa where they agreed to work together to preserve the peace in Europe. They condemned German rearmament. This became known as the Stresa Front against German aggression but it collapsed due to the Abyssinian crisis (see page 29), which destroyed close relations between France, Britain and Italy, and the Anglo-German Naval Treaty.

Anglo-German Naval Treaty, 1935

Hitler knew that Britain had some sympathy with Germany on the issue of rearmament. Britain believed that the limits imposed by the Treaty of Versailles were too tight and that a strong Germany was a buffer (barrier) against Communism. Indeed in 1935 Britain signed a naval agreement with Germany which allowed the Germans to build its navy up to 35 per cent of the size of the British navy and have the same number of submarines. Britain was accepting Hitler's breach of the Treaty of Versailles.

> **Exam tip** Candidates often have limited knowledge of German rearmament. Ensure you revise the key features of Hitler's policies in the years 1933–35.

The remilitarisation of the Rhineland, 1936

Hitler took further steps to reverse the Treaty of Versailles in March 1936 when he began moving German troops back into the Rhineland.

This was a calculated risk for Hitler because:
- the reoccupation of the Rhineland was a clear breach of the Versailles Treaty (see map on page 20)
- German troops were in no position to stand up to the French army if it reacted (Hitler's troops were under strict orders to retreat if this happened).

However, in 1936, France was occupied with domestic problems and Britain was not keen to provoke Germany. In addition, there was no doubt in Britain about the fairness of the Treaty of Versailles. The French were unwilling to act without the support of Britain, and so Hitler's gamble paid off.

This success convinced Hitler that Britain and France would not try to prevent him achieving his other aims. To many smaller nations, particularly those in eastern Europe, collective security seemed to have failed.

Making allies

Hitler was able to strengthen his position with a series of alliances:

Rome–Berlin Axis

This was signed with Mussolini, the dictator of Italy, in 1936 and was an informal agreement to co-operate. However, it was the beginning of closer relations between the two dictators who both provided support for the Nationalists in the Spanish Civil War.

The Anti-Comintern Pact

This was signed by Germany, Japan and Italy in 1937. They said they would work together to oppose Communism.

The Pact of Steel

This was a formal alliance between Italy and Germany which was signed in 1939 in which they agreed to support each other in a future war.

> ## Comment
>
> *This was the beginning of the controversial policy of appeasement. Britain and France certainly did not want war. They felt that they were not strong enough to go to war and were therefore prepared to give Hitler what he wanted.*

Revision tasks

1 Make a copy of the following table and briefly complete each box.

	Who between	What agreed
Rome–Berlin Axis		
Anti-Comintern Pact		
Pact of Steel		

2 Draw a flow chart to show the key features of Hitler's policies in the years 1933–36.

3 Explain why Hitler was successful in challenging the Treaty of Versailles in the years 1933–35.

> **Exam tip: q3** This is a Unit 1 style question. You will need to:
> - identify at least three reasons
> - make links between each of these reasons
> - prioritise the reasons. In other words explain which you think was the most important and why.

3.3 The failure of appeasement, 1937–39

From 1935 to 1938, Britain and France tried, unsuccessfully, to prevent further German expansion through a policy known as appeasement – that is, giving in to demands made by Hitler when they were thought to be reasonable.

Appeasement

The policy of appeasement is closely associated with Neville Chamberlain, who was British Prime Minister from 1937 to 1940. Britain believed that the Treaty of Versailles had been too harsh on Germany and that Hitler was justified in trying to undo its worst terms.

Hitler was convinced that appeasement meant that Britain and France would do nothing to stop him expanding his territories, especially as they had allowed him to build up his armed forces and reoccupy the Rhineland.

The *Anschluss* with Austria, 1938

Hitler had been born in Austria and one of his objectives was to see Germany and Austria as one country. By 1938, Hitler felt ready to try.

- Hitler bullied the Austrian Chancellor, Schuschnigg, into accepting a Nazi, Seyss-Inquart, as Austrian Minister of the Interior.
- Schuschnigg ordered a plebiscite to be held to find out if the Austrian people really wanted union with Germany.
- Hitler feared a 'no' vote, so he moved German troops to the Austrian border, and threatened to invade if Schuschnigg did not resign in favour of Seyss-Inquart.
- Seyss-Inquart became Chancellor and invited German troops into Austria. On 12 March 1938, the troops entered Vienna. The *Anschluss* was complete.
- The Nazis organised their own vote about union with Germany and, of those who voted, 99 per cent voted in favour. Austria immediately became a province of the new German Reich (empire).

The *Anschluss* with Austria was another clear breach of the Versailles Treaty. The British and French Governments complained about the German violation of the Treaty of Versailles but took no action.

> **Key terms**
>
> **Anschluss:** means union between Austria and Germany.

> **Comment**
>
> *Again, there was a feeling among some people in Britain that the Treaty of Versailles had been harsh and Britain should not defend it.*

The Sudeten crisis and Munich Agreement, 1938

Encouraged by his successes, Hitler took his plans a stage further and began to set his sights on Czechoslovakia, a new state set up after the First World War.

The Sudeten crisis

Part of Czechoslovakia consisted of German-speaking peoples in the area known as the Sudetenland. It was this area that next received Hitler's attention.

- Hitler ordered Henlein (the leader of the Sudeten Germans) to stir up trouble in the Sudetenland.
- German newspapers produced allegations of crimes apparently committed by Czechs against Sudeten Germans.
- Hitler threatened war if a solution was not found.

On 22 September, at a meeting at Godesberg, the Czech President Beneš refused to accept the German demands. It seemed that war was a real possibility, but Chamberlain appealed to Hitler to give him more time to find a settlement.

The Munich Agreement

On 29 September, Chamberlain made one last effort to maintain peace.
- He met with the French Prime Minister Daladier, Hitler and Mussolini at Munich in a last bid to resolve the Sudeten crisis.
- The Czech representatives were not invited to the meeting.
- The Czechs were forced to hand over the Sudetenland to Germany and a commission was set up to decide which territory the Czechs would lose.

Chamberlain and Hitler had a further meeting in Munich in which both men agreed that Britain and Germany would not go to war. Hitler promised he did not want the rest of Czechoslovakia. Chamberlain returned to Britain a hero, apparently having saved Europe from war.

The results of the Munich Agreement were extremely serious for Czechoslovakia and Europe as a whole.
- The Czech Government was completely humiliated.
- The vital area of the Sudetenland was lost and, in October and November 1938, Hungary and Poland also occupied other parts of Czech territory.
- Britain and France had again given in to Hitler.

> ## Comment
> *Although the Munich Agreement was initially seen as a success, it marked the end of Chamberlain's appeasement policy. After Munich, few people believed that Hitler could be trusted again. Britain and France increased the pace of their rearmament programme.*

Revision tasks

1 Make a copy of the following table and complete each box in five words or fewer.

	Causes	Events	Results
Anschluss			
Sudeten crisis			

2 In fewer than five words, explain the consequences of the Munich Agreement for each of the following countries.
   - Britain   • Germany   • Czechoslovakia

3 The Czechs felt they had been betrayed. Do you agree?

4 Describe one way in which Britain and France gave way to Hitler in the years 1937–38.

Exam tip: q4 This is a Unit 1 question. You only need to write two sentences.

The road to war

Chamberlain believed that he had achieved peace. Less than a year later, war had broken out.

Czechoslovakia, March 1939

In March 1939, Czechoslovakia finally disappeared from the map of Europe.
- Hitler invaded what was left of Czechoslovakia.
- Bohemia and Moravia became German protectorates (controlled by Germany).
- Slovakia remained independent in theory, but was dominated by Germany.
- Ruthenia was handed over to Hungary.

The end of appeasement

The final occupation of Czechoslovakia suggested that war was on its way.

- Hitler's promises made at Munich were clearly worthless.
- Britain and France were rapidly rearming and it was accepted that the policy of appeasement had failed.

Poland, 1939

Poland was Hitler's next target. In the Treaty of Versailles, German territory had been handed over to the Poles to give them access to the Baltic Sea (the 'Polish Corridor') and the German city of Danzig had been put under the control of the League of Nations. Following his success in Czechoslovakia, Hitler demanded the return of Danzig and the Polish Corridor in March 1939.

The French and British Governments, humiliated by Munich and the events that followed, now acted decisively.

- In April, they gave guarantees of support against German aggression to the Polish, Greek and Romanian Governments.
- They increased production of arms and equipment.

The prospect of a future war over Poland now partly hinged on the attitude of the Soviet Government, Poland's neighbour on its eastern side. Britain and France tried to reach an agreement with Stalin. They hoped to entice him into an agreement to threaten Germany on her eastern frontier.

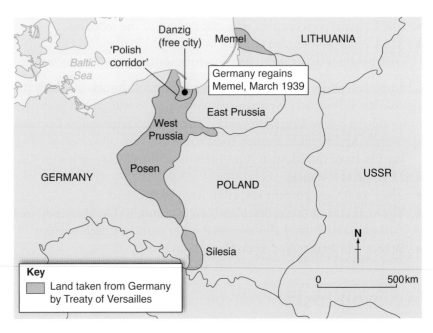

The Polish crisis, 1939.

The Nazi–Soviet Pact

In April 1939 Britain and France had guaranteed the frontiers of Poland against any attack. In fact, there was no way that they could help Poland if it had been attacked because of its distance from the West. The only country that could defend Poland against any German attack was the USSR. Britain and France began talks with the USSR to reach an agreement with it.

In 1939 Britain and France showed no urgency in making an agreement with the USSR. This made Stalin, the Soviet leader, more suspicious of their aims and led to him agreeing the Nazi–Soviet Pact with Hitler in August 1939.

On 23 August 1939, the German Foreign Minister, Ribbentrop, and Soviet Foreign Minister, Molotov, signed the Nazi–Soviet Non-Aggression Pact.

- The Soviets and Germans agreed not to fight each other in the event of war in Europe.
- Both powers secretly agreed to divide up Polish territory should war occur.
- Hitler gave Stalin a free hand to occupy part of Romania and the Baltic states of Latvia, Estonia and Lithuania.

The news of the Nazi–Soviet Non-Aggression Pact stunned the world because Hitler and Stalin represented two totally opposing political systems (Nazism and Communism). However, on closer inspection, the Nazi–Soviet Pact comes as less of a surprise. Despite their different political beliefs, Hitler and Stalin had much to offer each other.

Comment

Throughout the 1930s the Soviets felt that Britain had been trying to direct Hitler to the east, and it is true that there were many in Britain who feared Communism more than fascism. Evidence of this was the USSR's exclusion from the Munich Conference when clearly the future of Czechoslovakia was important to it.

- For Hitler, the pact removed the threat of war on two fronts. It also gave him the opportunity he needed to deal with Poland, despite the threats coming from Britain and France.
- Stalin had been suspicious of the British and French approaches – before the rise of Hitler they had shown little friendship to the USSR. Hitler, however, had more to offer the Soviets (for example, territory in eastern Europe).

Poland and the outbreak of war

Soon after the signing of the Nazi–Soviet Non-Aggression Pact, Hitler decided to invade Poland. What gave him the confidence to go ahead?

- The Pact allowed him to deal with the Polish problem without having to worry about a possible Soviet attack.
- The British and French guarantees of support for Poland in April 1939 were too late to convince him that they really were willing to go to war.
- The policy of appeasement had given him the impression that the British and French Governments would agree to almost anything in order to prevent another war with Germany.
- Even if war was declared, Poland was too far away for Britain and France to provide practical support. If war came, Hitler decided, it would be over very quickly and he would have achieved another of his objectives.

On 1 September 1939, German troops invaded Poland. Britain and France declared war soon after. On 15 September, the USSR also invaded Poland and took the territory agreed in the Nazi–Soviet Pact. Within six weeks, Poland had been defeated and, like Czechoslovakia, disappeared from the map of Europe.

> **Exam tip** The events of March–September 1939 are complex. Ensure you have a clear understanding of the sequence of events that led to war.

Appeasement: right or wrong?

It is easy with the use of hindsight to argue that British politicians such as Neville Chamberlain should have done more to prevent German aggression. However, many people in Britain and France agreed with the policy.

> **Exam tip** Do not simply criticise appeasement. Be aware of the arguments in favour of appeasement, especially that the majority of British people wanted to avoid another world war.

Reasons for appeasement	Reasons against appeasement
1 Many people remembered the horrors of the First World War and wanted to avoid war at all costs. 2 Many people believed that Germany had been treated too harshly by the Treaty of Versailles. 3 Some people saw Communism as the biggest threat to European stability. They thought that Germany could act as a buffer, especially as Hitler was very anti-Communist. 4 Britain was not ready for war. Rearmament started slowly in 1936, and the British forces were no match for the Germans in 1938. 5 Britain was preoccupied with the problems caused by the Depression, especially high unemployment, and wanted to stay out of unnecessary foreign involvement. 6 The events of the Spanish Civil War showed how powerful Germany, whose forces had intervened on the side of the Spanish leader, Franco, was and how horrific another war would be.	1 It gave Hitler the advantage. He grew stronger and stronger. When war came it was against a strong Germany. The war was fought in Poland, a country too far away for Britain to help. 2 It was not right: Britain and France allowed Hitler to break international agreements and especially the Treaty of Versailles. They were also prepared to give away parts of other countries, especially Czechoslovakia, to keep the peace. Appeasement was simply another word for weakness and cowardice. 3 Chamberlain misjudged Hitler. He believed Hitler was a rational man who would listen to reason. He did not realise, until it was too late, that appeasement simply encouraged Hitler to believe that he could do anything. 4 The appeasers missed excellent opportunities to stop Hitler, especially over the reoccupation of the Rhineland in 1936. 5 Appeasement did not stop war coming in 1939.

Revision tasks

1 Which do you think is the most powerful reason:
  a) in support of appeasement
  b) against appeasement?
  Explain your choices.

2 Draw a timeline with key details of each event from 1935–39 like the one below.

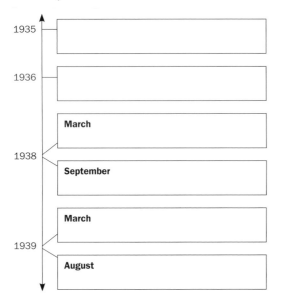

3 Draw a mind map showing the short-term reasons for the outbreak of war and the events of 1939. Your mind map should include the following reasons: the fall of Czechoslovakia, March 1939, the failure of appeasement, the Nazi–Soviet Pact, Poland.
  a) Put the reasons in order, clockwise, beginning with the most important at twelve o'clock.
  b) Briefly explain the most important reason.

4 Briefly explain the key features of the Nazi–Soviet Pact.

Exam tip: q4 This is a Unit 1 question. You will need to give at least three precise developed statements to achieve full marks.

Key content

You need to have a good working knowledge of the following areas:

- the impact of the Great Depression on international relations
- the causes, events and results of the Manchurian crisis, 1931–33
- the causes, events and results of the Abyssinian crisis, 1935–36
- Hitler's aims and policies including *Lebensraum* and *Grossdeutschland*
- Hitler and rearmament, 1933–35
- the Saar and the reoccupation of the Rhineland
- Hitler's alliances, especially the Rome–Berlin Axis and the Pact of Steel
- appeasement and the *Anschluss* with Austria
- the Sudeten crisis and the Munich Conference
- the takeover of Czechoslovakia, March 1939, and the Nazi–Soviet Pact
- the arguments for and against appeasement.

During the Second World War, the USA and the USSR had fought together as allies against Germany and Japan. Once this war was won, relations between the two 'superpowers' quickly deteriorated. A new war began – a war of ideas – and so it was known as the Cold War.

Key issues

As with all examination topics, you will be expected to do more than simply learn the content and write it out again. You will need to show understanding of key issues from the period. These are:

- Why did the Cold War begin?
- the development of the Cold War, 1945–48
- the development of the Cold War, 1948–56
- Hungary: the tightening of control.

4.1 Why did the Cold War begin?

The Cold War was a new kind of conflict, in which America and the USSR never declared war on each other. Instead there was a stand-off between the two superpowers which included an arms race and a propaganda war.

Conflicting ideologies

The two superpowers had very different **ideologies**.

The USA

What were the main political and economic features of the USA?
- It had a democratic system of government. The President and **Congress** of the USA were chosen in free democratic elections.
- It had a capitalist economy. Business and property were privately owned. Individuals could make profits in business or move jobs if they wished. However, they might also go bankrupt or lose their jobs.
- Americans believed firmly in the freedom of the individual and in government by consent.

In the 1920s and 1930s, the USA had followed a policy of **isolationism**. Now, faced by Communism extending into eastern Europe, the American Government was prepared to help and support people and countries who wanted democratic states with capitalist economies.

The USSR

The USSR was a Communist state.
- People could vote in elections for the **Supreme Soviet**, but they could only vote for members of the Communist Party and the Supreme Soviet had no real power. In the Communist system, people's lives were controlled closely.

Key terms

Ideology: a set of beliefs and characteristics.
Congress: the American representative assemblies (the equivalent of Parliament in Britain). There are two houses, the Senate and the House of Representatives.
Isolationism: withdrawing from international politics and policies.
Supreme Soviet: an elected body of representatives (the equivalent of the British Parliament), but which had no real power. It only met for two weeks a year. It was the Communist Party under Stalin that made the important decisions.

- The rights of individuals were seen as less important than the good of society as a whole.
- The USSR had a planned economy. The Government owned all industry and planned what every factory should produce.

Unlike the USA, the USSR had been attacked many times in the past. Germany had invaded Russia in 1914 and again in 1941. Stalin was determined that this would never happen again. In his view, the USSR could only be safe if the countries on its borders were controlled by Communist governments.

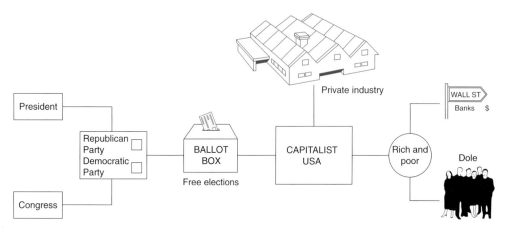

The main political and economic features of the USA.

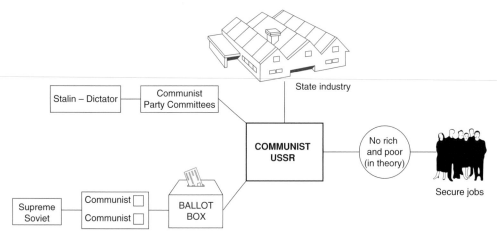

The main political and economic features of the USSR.

Revision tasks

1 Choose six key words to summarise the USA's system of government. Then choose six key words to summarise the USSR's system of government.

2 Compare the two in a table with the following headings:

USA	USSR

3 Describe one way in which the ideologies of the two superpowers differed in the years after 1945.

Exam tip: q3 This is a Unit 1 style question. You only need to write two sentences.

The breakdown of the Grand Alliance

This was set up in 1941 between Britain, the USA and the USSR to defeat Hitler and the Nazis. It was an alliance of convenience between three superpowers which had little in common.

The Teheran Conference, 1943

At the Teheran conference the Big Three – Stalin (leader of the USSR), Roosevelt (US President) and Churchill (British Prime Minister) – agreed that the Soviet Union could have a **'sphere of influence'** in Eastern Europe.

However, there were differences of opinion over Germany's future:

- Stalin wished to punish and severely weaken Germany with reparations
- Churchill and Roosevelt wanted to rebuild Germany. They remembered the mistakes of the Treaty of Versailles (see pages 20–21)

Key terms

'Sphere of influence': an area under Soviet control, which meant countries in Eastern Europe.

The Yalta Conference, February 1945

At the Yalta Conference, the Allied leaders (Churchill, Roosevelt and Stalin) got on well together. The following points were agreed.

- Germany would be divided into four zones. These would be run by the USA, France, Britain and the USSR.
- Germany's capital city, Berlin (which was in the Soviet zone), would also be divided into four zones.
- The countries of eastern Europe would be allowed to hold free elections to decide how they would be governed.
- The USSR would join in the war against Japan in return for territory in Manchuria and Sakhalin Island.

Exam tip Candidates often confuse the key features of these two conferences of 1945. Ensure you know who attended and what was agreed at each conference.

The Potsdam Conference, July–August 1945

In April 1945 President Roosevelt died, so at the Potsdam Conference the USA was represented by a new President, Harry Truman. During the conference, Churchill was replaced by Clement Attlee as British Prime Minister. The new leaders did not get on as well with Stalin as Roosevelt and Churchill had done.

There was agreement on some points of the discussions.

- The Nazi Party was to be banned and its leaders would be tried as war criminals.
- The Oder–Neisse (two rivers) line was to form part of the border between Poland and Germany.

However, there were disagreements on other issues. There were clear signs that Stalin did not trust the USA and Britain and that they did not trust him.

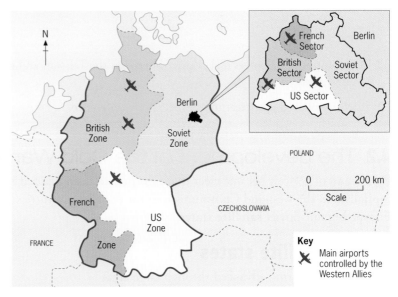

The division of Germany after the war.

Tensions at Potsdam

1 Britain and the USA denied Stalin a naval base in the Mediterranean.
- They saw no need for Stalin to have such a base.
- Stalin saw this as evidence that his allies mistrusted him.

2 Stalin wanted more reparations from Germany than Britain and the USA did.
- The USA and Britain did not wish to cripple Germany; they had seen the results of harsh reparations after the First World War.
- Stalin was suspicious about why his allies seemed to want to protect Germany and even help it recover.

Attlee   **Truman**   **Stalin**

3 Stalin had set up a Communist government in Lublin, the capital of Poland. Britain preferred the non-Communist Polish Government, which had lived in exile in Britain throughout the war. Truman and Attlee were very suspicious of Stalin's motives in setting up a Communist government.

The atom bomb further worsened relations between the USA and USSR during the Potsdam Conference. Stalin had been told about the atom bomb by Truman at the start of the Potsdam Conference and was furious that it had been kept a secret. The use of the atom bomb increased rivalry between the superpowers:

- Stalin was convinced that the USA was using the bombs as a warning to the USSR.
- Truman was convinced that the USA had the ultimate weapon and this made him even more determined to stand up to Stalin and prevent further Soviet expansion.
- An arms race emerged with the USSR determined to develop its own atom bomb.

Revision tasks

1 Make a copy of the following table and add notes on what was agreed/where there was disagreement.

Conference	Points agreed	Areas of disagreement
Teheran		
Yalta		
Potsdam		

2 What important changes had occurred between the Teheran and the Potsdam Conferences?

3 Briefly explain the key features of the Yalta Conference.

Exam tip: q3 This is a Unit 1 question. You will need to give at least three precise developed statements to achieve full marks.

4.2 The development of the Cold War, 1945–48

By the end of 1945 it became clear that Europe had been divided between capitalism in the west and Communism in the east. The countries of eastern Europe became Soviet **satellite states.**

Key terms

Satellite state: a country under the influence or control of another state.

Soviet satellite states

The Soviet Red Army advanced through large areas of eastern Europe whilst driving back the Germans. One year after the war, many Soviet troops were still stationed in much of eastern Europe.

Elections were held in each eastern European country, as promised at Yalta in 1945, but the evidence suggests that they were rigged to allow the USSR-backed Communist parties to take control. In Bulgaria, Albania, Poland, Romania and Hungary, opponents of the Communists were beaten, murdered or frightened into submission. By 1948, all eastern European states had Communist governments.

The spread of Communism, 1945–48.

Europe was now divided – East and West. In 1946, Churchill called this division the 'Iron Curtain'. He said:

From Stettin on the Baltic to Trieste on the Adriatic, an iron curtain has descended across the Continent. Behind that line lie all the capitals of Central and Eastern Europe … and all are subject to a very high measure of control from Moscow.

Revision tasks

1 What is meant by:
- the 'Iron Curtain'
- satellite states?

2 Make a copy of the table below and, in no more than one sentence, summarise the views of each side about Soviet expansion in eastern Europe.

Soviet view	
US view	

3 Explain why the USA and the USSR had become rivals by the end of 1946.

Comment
Stalin was simply carrying out his policy of making sure he had friendly governments on his doorstep. However, to the British and Americans, he seemed to be trying to build up a Communist empire.

Exam tip: q3 This is a Unit 1 style question. You will need to:
- identify at least three reasons
- make links between each of these reasons
- prioritise the reasons. In other words, explain which you think was the most important and why.

US involvement in Europe

In 1947 the USA committed itself to a policy of containment of Communism in Europe. Truman had received worrying news in the 'Long Telegram', a secret report from Kennan, America's ambassador in Moscow. The telegram suggested that Stalin was determined to destroy capitalism by building up his military power.

Greece

You can see from the map on page 40 that Greece appeared to be next in line in the spread of Communism. Greek resistance against the Germans had been divided into two movements – the royalists (who wanted the return of the king) and the Communists. After the war, the royalists restored the king with the help of British troops. However, they came under attack from Communist forces and asked the USA for help in early 1947.

Truman was already very worried about the spread of Communism. Under a foreign policy initiative that became known as the Truman **Doctrine**, the USA provided Greece with arms, supplies and money. The Communists were defeated in 1949 after a civil war.

The Truman Doctrine, 1947

Events in Greece convinced Truman that unless he acted, Communism would continue to spread. He therefore explained his policy to the world. This became known as the Truman Doctrine. Truman said:

I believe it must be the policy of the USA to support all free people who are resisting attempted subjugation by armed minorities or by outside pressure.

- The USA would not return to isolationism – it would play a leading role in the world.
- The aim was to contain (stop the spread of) Communism but not to push it back. This became the policy of **containment**.

Key terms
Doctrine: a statement of ideas.
Containment: a foreign policy aimed at containing the political influence or military power of another country – for example, US policy to stop the spread of Communism during the Cold War.

The Marshall Plan

The USA also became committed to the economic recovery of western Europe to prevent the spread of Communism.

Truman believed that poverty and hardship provided a breeding ground for Communism, so he wanted to make Europe prosperous again. It was also important for American businesses to have trading partners in the future, yet Europe's economies were still in ruins after the war.

The American Secretary of State, George Marshall, therefore visited Europe and came up with a European recovery programme – usually known as the Marshall Plan or Marshall Aid. This had two main aims:

- to stop the spread of Communism (Truman did not admit this at the time)
- to help the economies of Europe to recover (this would eventually provide a market for American exports).

Between 12 and 13 billion dollars poured into Europe in the years 1947–51, providing vital help for Europe's economic recovery. However, Marshall Aid also caused tensions:

- Only sixteen European countries accepted it – and these were all western European states.
- Stalin refused Marshall Aid for the USSR and banned eastern European countries from accepting it. Instead, he created his own organisations known as Cominform and Comecon.

The Soviet response

Cominform, 1947

In 1947, Stalin set up Cominform – an alliance of Communist countries – probably as a response to the Marshall Plan. Its aim was to spread Communist ideas, but it also helped Stalin tighten his hold on his Communist allies because it restricted their contact with the West.

Only one Communist leader, Marshall Tito of Yugoslavia, was not prepared to accept Stalin's total leadership. He split with Moscow. However, Yugoslavia remained Communist.

Comecon, 1949

Set up by Stalin to co-ordinate the production and trade of the eastern European countries, it was like an early Communist version of the European Community. However, Comecon favoured the USSR more than any of its other members.

Bizonia

By 1947, the British and American zones were operating as one and became 'Bizonia', meaning two zones. Bizonia and the French zone later became 'Trizonia'.

> ### Comment
>
> *Marshall Aid was a generous gesture by the USA but it was not entirely an act of kindness. Stalin saw it as an attempt by American business to dominate western Europe. If the USA was determined to 'buy' western Europe with its dollars, then he was determined to control eastern Europe with his Communist allies and the Red Army.*

> **Exam tip** Candidates often confuse the Truman Doctrine and the Marshall Plan. Ensure you have a thorough knowledge of both. Remember the Truman Doctrine is about political aid to western Europe to contain the spread of Communism and the Marshall Plan is economic aid.

Revision tasks

1 The Truman Doctrine and the Marshall Plan were described as being two sides of the same coin. Make your own copy of both sides of this imaginary coin, big enough to write in. On one side give a brief definition of the Truman Doctrine. On the other side write a brief definition of the Marshall Plan.

2 How far do you feel each side was to blame for the tension after the Second World War? Decide where you would put the USA and the USSR on the scale below:

Mostly to blame ⟵——————————⟶ Not to blame

3 Briefly explain the key features of the Marshall Plan.

> **Exam tip: q3** This is a Unit 1 question. You will need to give at least three precise developed statements to achieve full marks.

4.3 The development of the Cold War, 1948–56

The Cold War intensified in the years after 1948 due to the Berlin Crisis of 1948–49, the formation of rival alliance systems and the nuclear arms race.

The Berlin blockade and airlift, 1948–49

This was the first major crisis of the Cold War.

Causes

Germany's economy and government had been shattered by the war and the Allies were faced with a serious question: should they continue to occupy Germany or should they try to rebuild it?

- Britain and the USA wanted Germany to recover – they could not afford to keep feeding its people and they felt that punishing Germany would not help future peace.
- The USSR did not want to rebuild Germany and Stalin was suspicious about why the USA and Britain did.

In 1948, the French, American and British zones merged to become one zone, 'Trizonia' (in August 1949 this area became known as West Germany). With the help of Marshall Aid, West Germany began to recover and prosper. It was a very different story in East Germany. In this area, controlled by the USSR, there was poverty and hunger. Many East Germans were leaving because West Germany seemed a much more attractive place to live.

In Stalin's eyes, it seemed that the Allies were building up West Germany in order to attack him. When in 1948 they introduced a new West German currency (the Deutsche Mark), it was the last straw.

Events

Stalin tried to **blockade** Berlin, the former capital of Germany, in East Germany (see map on page 39). In a month, he closed all road and rail connections from Berlin to West Germany, hoping he could force the western Allies out of the city. For many people at the time, it seemed there was a real risk of war. The USA and Britain faced a choice:

- they could withdraw – but this would be humiliating and it might encourage Stalin to think he could invade West Germany
- they could lift supplies into West Berlin by air – they had the planes but it would be risky as they might be shot down.

The Allies decided to airlift supplies. The airlift lasted until the following Spring of 1949 and reached its peak on 16–17 April when 1,398 flights landed nearly 13,000 tonnes of supplies in 24 hours. During the airlift West Berliners were supplied with everything from food and clothing to oil and building supplies. It was a great success.

Results

By May 1949, the USSR lifted the blockade. It was a victory for the West, but relations with the USSR hit rock bottom. Co-operation in Germany in the future was very unlikely and the country would remain divided. The zone controlled by the USA, Britain and France became the Federal Republic of Germany (West Germany) in August 1949. In October 1949, the Soviet zone became the German Democratic Republic (East Germany).

Key terms

Blockade: the surrounding of a place with troops or ships to prevent the entry or exit of supplies.

Revision task

Draw a flow chart to show the causes, events and results of the Berlin crisis of 1948–49.

Exam tip Candidates often confuse this crisis with the crisis over the Berlin Wall in 1961. An easy way to remember the difference is 'B' for blockade comes before 'W' for wall.

Rival alliances

By 1956 there were two rival alliance systems each dominated by one of the superpowers.

NATO (North Atlantic Treaty Organisation), 1949

This military alliance contained most of the states in western Europe as well as the USA and Canada. Its main purpose was to defend its members. If one member was attacked, the other members would help to defend it. When the USSR developed its own atomic bomb in 1949, NATO seemed even more important to the defence of western Europe, since at the time no western European country had atomic weapons.

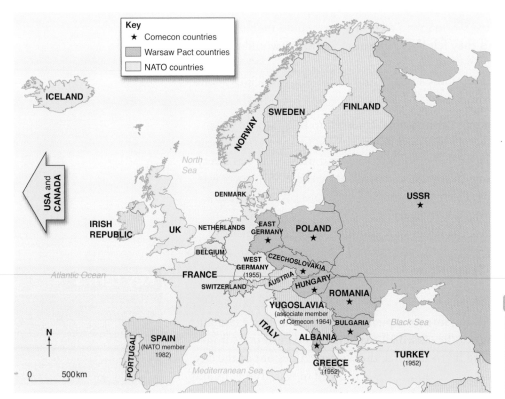

Alliances, 1949–55.

Exam tip Questions on NATO are often not well answered as candidates fail to revise its features and importance. Ensure you revise these thoroughly.

The importance of NATO

- The USA was now formally committed to the defence of western Europe.
- Stalin did not see it as a defensive alliance but as a direct threat to the USSR.
- The USA was able to build air bases in western Europe where planes armed with nuclear weapons could be stationed ready for use against the Soviet Union.

The Warsaw Pact

In 1955, West Germany joined NATO. The Soviet response was to set up the Warsaw Pact – a Communist version of NATO. The Soviets had not forgotten the damage that Germany had inflicted on the USSR in the Second World War.

The nuclear arms race

- During 1945–49, the USA was the only country to possess atomic weapons.
- In 1949, the USSR successfully tested an atomic bomb.
- In 1952, the USA detonated its first hydrogen bomb.
- In 1953, the USSR tested its own hydrogen bomb.

Comment

All of the alliances demonstrated the fear and mistrust that brought about the Cold War. The western democracies and the USSR both feared the rise of another state like Nazi Germany. However, each side saw the other as this potential threat, certainly not itself. The creation of alliances for self-defence on one side could very easily look like an alliance preparing to attack the other side.

By 1953, the USSR appeared to be catching up with the USA in the developing arms race. The balance tilted even more in the direction of the USSR when China became Communist in October 1949. In 1950, Stalin and the new Chinese Communist leader, Mao Zedong, signed a 30-year treaty of friendship.

In 1957, the arms race moved into a new phase with the development of satellites. These meant that nuclear bombs would no longer have to be dropped from long-range aircraft but could be launched out of the Earth's atmosphere and guided towards a target. In 1957, the USSR used a rocket to launch Sputnik I into orbit around the Earth. The Americans developed their own rockets. The 'space race' had begun.

Both countries then developed ICBMs (Inter-Continental Ballistic Missiles), which were long-range missiles that could be launched from underground bases. The USA also created Polaris missiles, which could be fired from a submarine, with a range of over 1,600 kilometres. The USSR developed its own version.

> ### Comment
> *The Polaris missile was a Submarine-Launched Ballistic Missile (SLBM) carrying a nuclear warhead developed during the Cold War for the US Navy. It was gradually replaced by the Poseidon missile from 1972 onwards.*

Revision tasks

1 Make a copy of the table below. Use the information in this chapter to complete it.

Organisation	Members	Purpose	Effects on East–West relations
Marshall Plan			
Comecon			
Cominform			
NATO			
Warsaw Pact			

2 Put the following events of the Cold War in chronological order with the year they took place.
   - Setting up of NATO
   - Teheran Conference
   - 'Iron Curtain' Speech
   - Potsdam Conference
   - Marshall Plan
   - Berlin Crisis
   - Setting up of Warsaw Pact
   - Yalta Conference
   - Truman Doctrine

4.4 Hungary: the tightening of control

In 1956, an attempted uprising was brutally crushed by the USSR.

The uprising

Causes

Hungary had been treated as a defeated country by the Soviets after the Second World War and, with the support of the USSR, a Communist government had been established under its leader, Mátyás Rákosi, who closely followed Stalin's rules. The Hungarians hated Rákosi and his secret police (the AVH) because of the brutality they had shown, executing or imprisoning thousands of opponents. There were protests against the falling standard of living and increased poverty, which they blamed on Soviet policies.

Events

The protests got worse and Stalin's statue was pulled down and dragged through the streets. Rákosi was forced to resign and Soviet tanks moved in. Imre Nagy became Prime Minister and the Soviet troops withdrew. Nagy was determined on reform. He wanted free elections, the end of the secret police and the removal of the Soviet army of occupation.

However, Khrushchev became alarmed when Nagy demanded the right for Hungary to withdraw from the Warsaw Pact and follow a neutral role in the Cold War. This was too much for the USSR. Free elections could mean the end of Communism in Hungary. If Hungary withdrew from the Warsaw Pact, there would be a gap in the Iron Curtain; the Soviet buffer zone with the West would be broken.

Soviet troops and 1,000 tanks moved into Hungary to crush the uprising. Nagy appealed to the West for help but none came. Two weeks of fighting followed but the Hungarians were no match for the Soviet forces. Nagy was captured, then shot.

Results

- Between 2,500 and 30,000 Hungarians, mostly civilians, were killed along with 700 Soviet troops. Over 200,000 refugees fled Hungary and settled in the West.
- The uprising highlighted the limitations of Khrushchev's policy of **peaceful co-existence**.
- There was no active support for the uprising in the West. This was because Britain, France and the USA were preoccupied with the Suez Crisis.
- A new pro-Soviet government was set up under János Kádár. Kádár re-established Communist control of Hungary and negotiated the withdrawal of Soviet troops once the crisis was over.
- Other satellite states in eastern Europe did not dare to challenge Soviet authority after the events in Hungary.

Comment

The Suez crisis was a war fought by Britain, France and Israel against Egypt in October 1956. It followed the decision by President Nasser of Egypt to nationalise the Suez Canal. Both the USA and the USSR objected to the attack on Egypt and forced Britain, France and Israel to withdraw.

Revision tasks

1 Describe one cause of the Hungarian uprising of 1956.

2 Make a copy of the table below and summarise the part played by each person in the Hungarian uprising.

Nagy	
Khrushchev	
Kádár	
Rákosi	

3 Draw a timeline for the years 1945–56. On the timeline:
   a) include the key events of the Cold War
   b) briefly explain how each event worsened relations between the two superpowers.

Exam tip: q1 This is a Unit 1 style question. You only need two sentences in your answer.

Key content

You need to have a good working knowledge of the following areas:

- the Teheran, Yalta and Potsdam Conferences
- the ideological differences between the superpowers and the concept of the 'Iron Curtain'
- the establishment and control of the Soviet satellite states
- Cominform and Comecon
- the Truman Doctrine and the Marshall Plan
- the causes, events and results of the Berlin crisis of 1948–49
- NATO and the Warsaw Pact
- the nuclear arms race
- the causes, events and results of the Hungarian uprising of 1956.

The Cold War intensified in the 1960s with three crises: the Berlin Wall in 1961, the Cuban Missile Crisis in 1962, and Czechoslovakia in 1968.

Key issues

As with all examination topics, you will be expected to do more than simply learn the content and write it out again. You will need to show understanding of key issues from the period. These are:

- Berlin: a divided city
- Cuba: the world on the brink of war
- Czechoslovakia: the Prague Spring.

5.1 Berlin: a divided city

In 1961 the Cold War reached another turning point with the construction of the Berlin Wall.

The situation in Berlin

Berlin had always been a source of conflict between the Soviets and western Allies. Capitalist West Berlin, surrounded by the Communist state of East Germany, continued to be a problem for East Germany and the USSR.

- The high standard of living enjoyed by the people of West Berlin contrasted sharply with that of the Communist half of the city – East Berlin. It was a continual reminder to the people in East Germany of their poor living conditions.
- It was estimated that 3 million people had crossed from East to West Berlin between 1946 and 1960. Many of these people were skilled workers and it seemed that the economic survival of East Germany was in doubt if this escape route remained open.

The building of the Wall

In 1961, Khrushchev and the East German leadership decided to act. Without warning, on 13 August 1961, the East Germans began to build a wall surrounding West Berlin.

- At first, the structure was little more than a barbed wire fence, but by 17 August it was replaced with a stone wall.
- All movement between East and West Berlin was stopped.
- For several days, Soviet and American tanks faced each other across divided Berlin streets.

The building of the Berlin Wall had some immediate effects.

- The flow of refugees was reduced to a trickle.
- Western nations won a propaganda victory since it appeared that Communist states needed to build walls to prevent their citizens from leaving.

However, the western nations had to be satisfied with a propaganda victory only. It was clear that the USA and NATO were not going to try to stop the building of the Wall. In reality, there was little the western powers could do to stop it.

Kennedy's response

From the 1960s until the 1980s, the Berlin Wall became a symbol of the division between the capitalist West and the communist East. American President John F. Kennedy made a historic visit to West Berlin in 1963 and declared that the city was a symbol of the struggle between the forces of freedom and the Communist world. For the USSR and East Germany, however, the wall was simply an economic and political necessity. The loss of so many refugees from East Germany had been threatening the very existence of the state.

> **Exam tip** Candidates often confuse this crisis with the crisis over the Berlin blockade in 1948. An easy way to remember the difference is 'B' for blockade comes before 'W' for wall.

Revision tasks

1 Why was Khrushchev so determined to force the USA out of West Berlin?

2 What were the effects of the construction of the Berlin Wall?

3 Briefly explain the key features of the Berlin crisis of 1961.

> **Exam tip: q3** This is a Unit 1 question. You will need to give at least three precise developed statements to achieve full marks.

5.2 Cuba: the world on the brink of war

The Cuban missile crisis was the most serious conflict between the USSR and the USA in the history of the Cold War. Cuba was a Communist country just 144 kilometres off the coast of the USA. In October 1962, American spy planes identified nuclear missile sites being built on Cuba.

Castro and Cuba

Cuba had become Communist after a takeover by Fidel Castro in 1958. He was popular in Cuba, in part because he gave land seized from wealthy Americans to the Cuban people.

The USA had retaliated by cutting off aid to Cuba, and refused to buy Castro's cotton and tobacco. In return, Castro secured help from the USSR. Khrushchev was keen to gain influence in Cuba, close to the USA's south-eastern coastline.

In spring 1961, the USA had a new President, John F. Kennedy. He was alarmed at what he saw as a Communist threat on the USA's doorstep. He gave American support to an invasion of Cuba by rebels opposed to Castro's Government. The landing took place at the Bay of Pigs, and was a disaster. There was no popular support for it in Cuba.

> ### Comment
>
> *In some ways, the Cuban missile crisis was the height of Cold War tension. Never before had the world been so close to nuclear conflict as it was in October 1962. However, the crisis resulted in arms reductions and improved communications (if not better relations) between the USA and the USSR.*

Events of the crisis, 1962

The position and threat of Cuban missiles, and the crisis at its peak, October 1962.

The crisis lasted for thirteen days.

16 October	Kennedy was told that Khrushchev intended to build missile sites in Cuba.
18–19 October	Kennedy held talks with his closest advisers. The 'Hawks' wanted an aggressive policy whilst the 'Doves' favoured a peaceful solution.
20 October	Kennedy decided to impose a naval **blockade** around Cuba to prevent Soviet missiles and equipment reaching Cuba. The Americans searched any ship suspected of carrying arms or missiles.
21 October	Kennedy made a broadcast to the American people, informing them of the potential threat and what he intended to do.
23 October	Khrushchev sent a letter to Kennedy insisting that Soviet ships would force their way through the blockade.
24 October	Khrushchev issued a statement insisting that the Soviet Union would use nuclear weapons in the event of a war.
25 October	Kennedy wrote to Khrushchev asking him to withdraw missiles from Cuba.
26 October	Khrushchev replied to Kennedy's letter. He said he would withdraw the missiles if the USA promised not to invade Cuba and withdraw its missiles from Turkey.
27 October	A US spy plane was shot down over Cuba. Attorney General Robert Kennedy (brother of the President) proposed a deal with the Soviet Union. The USA would withdraw missiles from Turkey as long as it was kept secret.
28 October	Khrushchev accepted the deal.

Results of the crisis

The Cuban crisis had a major effect on East–West relations.

- Leaders of both the USSR and the USA realised that nuclear war had been a real possibility and it was vital that a similar crisis should not happen again.
- The Americans and Soviets decided to set up a telephone link (or 'hot line') so that direct communication could take place in future between Washington and Moscow. Nuclear arms talks also began and, in 1963, a Test Ban Treaty was signed between the USA, the USSR and Britain.

Key terms

Blockade: the surrounding of a place with troops or ships to prevent the entry or exit of supplies.

Revision tasks

1 Make a copy of the table below and summarise the part played by each person in the Cuban missile crisis.

Castro	
John Kennedy	
Robert Kennedy	
Khrushchev	

2 Place the following events of the crisis in chronological order.
- an American U-2 plane is shot down over Cuba
- the USA blockade Cuba
- Khrushchev accepts the deal
- the US discover Soviet missile sites on Cuba
- Robert Kennedy suggests a deal.

3 Which country do you think gained the most from the crisis: the USA, the USSR or Cuba? Explain your answer.

4 Explain why there was a crisis over Cuba in 1962.

Exam tip The Cuban missile crisis is a popular exam topic. Ensure you thoroughly revise the causes, events and results.

Exam tip: q4 This is a Unit 1 style question. You will need to:
- identify at least three reasons
- make links between each of these reasons
- prioritise the reasons. In other words, explain which you think was the most important and why.

5.3 Czechoslovakia: the Prague Spring, 1968

In 1968 the USSR once again showed its unwillingness to allow greater freedom in the Eastern Bloc.

In 1967, Alexander Dubček had become Communist Party Secretary in Czechoslovakia. In the spring of 1968 (the 'Prague Spring'), Dubček began to reform the Communist system.

- Censorship of the press was ended.
- Other political parties apart from the Communist Party were allowed.
- Some political prisoners were released and Czech citizens were given greater freedom to travel abroad.

The reforms in Czechoslovakia became known as 'Communism with a human face'. They seemed to represent the general easing of tension between East and West that had taken place after the Cuban crisis.

Soviet reaction

However, Dubček's reforms were seen as a major threat by the new leader of the USSR, Brezhnev. As in Hungary twelve years earlier, action was taken to prevent the reforms from sweeping the Communists out of power in Czechoslovakia and spreading to the rest of eastern Europe.

- In August 1968, 400,000 Warsaw Pact troops entered Czechoslovakia, arrested leading reformers and seized key towns and cities.
- Dubček and the Czech President Svoboda were flown to Moscow where they talked with Brezhnev for four days.
- On 27 August, the Czech leaders returned and announced that many of their reforms were to be stopped and censorship reintroduced. In 1969 Dubček resigned and was replaced by a loyal Communist, Husak.

Reaction from the rest of the world

America was fighting a bloody war against Communism in Vietnam. It knew that Brezhnev would not interfere in Vietnam if the USA did not intervene in Czechoslovakia. The western European governments followed America's lead. They condemned the invasion but did nothing.

However, the Soviet invasion did lead to discontent in eastern Europe. Yugoslavia and Romania condemned the invasion and formed alliances with China, the other major Communist power and now a rival of the USSR.

The Brezhnev Doctrine

After the failure of the Czechs to gain more freedom from Soviet control, the new Czech leader, Husak, set about returning to the old ways. The reforms of the Prague Spring were reversed, and the USSR was once more firmly in control of Czech policy.

Brezhnev then set out what became known as the Brezhnev Doctrine. He argued that a threat to one socialist (that is, Communist) country was a threat to them all. (This doctrine clearly echoed the Truman Doctrine of 1947 and the American fear of the domino effect.) However, he went on to say that force would be used whenever necessary to keep the Soviet satellites firmly under Soviet influence.

This doctrine and the Soviet actions in Czechoslovakia in 1968 did nothing to improve relations between the USSR and the USA. Yet, in spite of it, there was a thaw in relations very quickly in what has become known as the process of **Détente**.

Comment

The end of the Prague Spring showed once again that the Soviet leadership would not tolerate reform in its satellite states and that the West was unwilling to risk nuclear war over eastern European countries.

Key terms

Détente: the relaxing of tension or hostility between nations – for example, the improvement of relations between the USA and the USSR at the end of the 1960s.

Revision tasks

1 Explain briefly the key features of the Prague Spring.

2 Describe one consequence of the Soviet invasion of Czechoslovakia.

3 Make a copy of the table below. Use the information in this chapter to complete it. Write in note form and be concise.

Crises	Causes	Effects
1 Berlin crisis, 1961		
American view		
Soviet view		
2 Cuban missile crisis		
American view		
Soviet view		
3 Czechoslovakia		
American view		
Soviet view		

4 Which of the three crises was the most serious threat to world peace? Give reasons for your decision.

Exam tip: q1 This is a Unit 1 question. You will need to give at least three precise developed statements to achieve full marks.

Exam tip: q2 This is a Unit 1 style question. You only need to write two sentences.

Key content

You need to have a good working knowledge of the following areas:

- the reasons for the building of the Berlin Wall, including the refugee problem and the failure of the summit conferences
- the construction of the Berlin Wall and its effects on East–West relations
- Kennedy's reaction to the Wall and his visit to Berlin, 1963
- the causes of the Cuban missile crisis, including Castro and the USSR and the Bay of Pigs
- the events of the crisis and how it was resolved
- short- and long-term effects of the missile crisis
- opposition to Soviet control of Czechoslovakia and the Prague Spring
- Soviet reactions and the invasion of Czechoslovakia
- the Brezhnev Doctrine and its effects.

Chapter 6: Why did the Cold War end? The invasion of Afghanistan to the collapse of the Soviet Union, 1979–91

The final part of the Cold War started with the Russian invasion of Afghanistan and President Reagan's reference to the Soviet Union as 'that evil empire'. Yet within a few years relations were improving. Then, suddenly, at the end of the 1980s the USSR started to lose control of its satellite countries and by 1991 the USSR had disintegrated. The Cold War was over.

Key issues

As with all examination topics, you will be expected to do more than simply learn the content and write it out again. You will need to show understanding of key issues from the period. These are:

- the collapse of Détente – the effects of the Soviet invasion of Afghanistan, 1979
- President Reagan and the US reaction
- President Gorbachev and the end of the Cold War.

6.1 The collapse of Détente

The 1970s was a decade associated with **Détente**. There was more contact between leaders and a number of international agreements were made on a range of issues. This ended with the Soviet invasion of Afghanistan and was followed by what became known as the second Cold War.

Détente

Détente meant a general easing of tension in relations between the superpowers. The high point of Détente was the Helsinki Conference of 1975.

Strategic Arms Limitation Talks (SALT)

In 1969, the USA and the USSR began negotiations in an effort to control the arms race. The talks lasted for three years and in 1972 **SALT** I was signed. Both sides agreed to keep the number of nuclear weapons and warheads within strict limits. They also agreed to begin further talks to discuss weapons systems not included in SALT I.

Co-operation in space

Throughout the 1960s, the Americans and Soviets had been arch rivals in the 'space race'. Yet in July 1975, three American astronauts and two Soviet cosmonauts docked their Apollo and Soyuz spacecraft together in orbit around the Earth. It was one of the most visible signs of Détente in action and gave a further impetus to superpower co-operation.

The Helsinki Conference, August 1975

In August 1975 at Helsinki in Finland, 35 countries, including the USSR and the USA, signed the Helsinki Agreement. This was a high point for Détente.

> ### Key terms
>
> **Détente:** the relaxing of tension or hostility between nations – for example, the improvement of relations between the USA and the USSR at the end of the 1960s.
>
> **SALT:** Strategic Arms Limitation Talks, which limited the number of nuclear weapons and warheads held by each side.

- The western powers recognised the frontiers of eastern Europe and Soviet influence in that area.
- West Germany officially recognised East Germany.
- The Soviets agreed to buy American grain and to export oil to the West.
- The Soviets agreed to allow greater freedom in the Soviet Union to western journalists, to give 21 days' notice before holding military manoeuvres near to a frontier, and to allow some inspection of human rights.
- All countries agreed to improve human rights throughout the world.

It should be remembered that these resolutions were not always put into force. For example, abuses of human rights continued in the USSR and other countries after 1975.

> **Exam tip** Détente is the least well known period of the Cold War. Ensure you know what it means and its key features.

Revision task

Make a copy of the following table and summarise the key features of Détente.

The meaning of détente	
SALT	
Co-operation in space	
The Helsinki Conference	

The Soviet invasion of Afghanistan

The 1970s saw improving relations between the superpowers. However, these were damaged once again by the USSR's invasion of Afghanistan in 1979. The Soviets insisted that they had been invited into Afghanistan to restore order, but western nations protested that it was a straightforward invasion that could not be justified. Despite worldwide protests, the invasion and occupation of Afghanistan continued.

> **Key terms**
>
> **Mujahidin:** Afghan Muslim freedom fighters who fought against the Soviet occupation using guerrilla tactics.

Reasons for the invasion

The Soviets invaded Afghanistan for several reasons.
- They were concerned about the Muslim revolution in neighbouring Iran, which could have spread to Afghanistan and Muslim areas inside the USSR.
- The political situation in Afghanistan was very unstable at the end of the 1970s and the Soviets wanted to maintain their influence in the area.
- Afghanistan was close to the Middle East oil reserves of the western powers and the ports of the Indian Ocean. The Soviets wanted to develop their interests in this area.

Consequences

Within weeks of the invasion, Soviet troops were being killed by **Mujahidin** rebels who used very effective guerrilla tactics. The USA secretly began to send very large shipments of money, arms and equipment to Pakistan and from there to the Mujahidin. The campaign became a nightmare for the USSR; unwinnable and a severe drain on its finances.

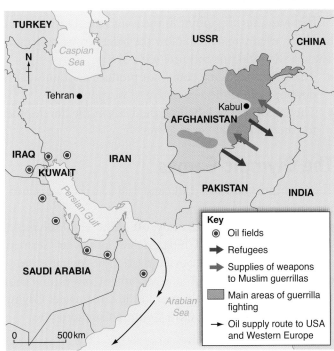

The importance of Afghanistan to the Soviets.

The Carter Doctrine

Following the Soviet invasion, Carter made a statement that became known as the Carter **Doctrine.** The doctrine said that the USA would not allow the USSR to gain control of territory in the oil-rich Middle East.

Carter's actions

President Carter was furious with the Soviet invasion and took action. He pulled the USA out of the 1980 Moscow Olympic Games. (The USSR retaliated in 1984 by pulling out of the Los Angeles Games, see below.) Carter told the Senate not to ratify (agree to) the SALT II treaty that was ready to sign and would have further limited the number of nuclear weapons. He also cut trade between the USA and the USSR – for example, he prevented food and technological goods, such as computers, being sold to the USSR. He also formed an alliance with China and Israel to support the Afghan rebels, providing weapons and funds for the Mujahidin.

> **Exam tip** The Soviet invasion of Afghanistan is one of the most important turning points in the Cold War. It brought an end to détente and the resumption of the Cold War.

6.2 President Reagan and the US reaction

The period following the Soviet invasion of Afghanistan is often described as the Second Cold War.

The 'evil empire'

Ronald Reagan succeeded Carter as President of the USA. He believed that Détente had been a disaster and rejected the idea of **peaceful co-existence** with the USSR. Instead he was determined to get tough and in a speech in 1983 referred to the USSR as 'that evil empire'.

> ### Key terms
>
> **Doctrine:** a statement of ideas.
> **Peaceful co-existence:** the policy of co-operation rather than rivalry with the West.
> **Boycott:** to refuse to take part in.

'Star Wars'

Reagan was convinced that the USA could win the Cold War. He believed that the USSR should be forced to disarm by his new initiative – SDI (the Strategic Defence Initiative) which was nicknamed 'Star Wars'. It was intended to be a satellite anti-missile system that would orbit the earth to protect the USA from any Soviet missiles. Satellites equipped with powerful lasers would act as a 'nuclear umbrella' against Soviet nuclear weapons.

This was a turning point in the arms race. During détente the two superpowers had been evenly matched. Now the balance was very much in favour of the USA. The USSR could not compete with SDI.

- The Soviet economy could not produce enough wealth to finance the development of new space-based weapons.
- The USSR was well behind the USA in the development of computers, essential for the 'Star Wars' programme.

> **Exam tip** Candidates often lack precise knowledge of the key developments in the Cold War in the years 1979–84. Ensure you revise this section thoroughly.

The Olympic Games

The Olympic Games of 1980 and 1984 further worsened relations between the two superpowers.

- President Carter led the **boycott** of the 1980 Olympics in Moscow. Sixty countries, including China, Malawi and West Germany, did the same as a sign of protest against the Soviet invasion of Afghanistan.
- The Soviet Union and fourteen other Communist countries retaliated four years later by refusing to take part in the Los Angeles Olympics. The USSR organised the Friendship Games as a Communist alternative.

Revision tasks

1 Make a copy of this table. Complete it in note form and be concise.

Development	Key features	Why it worsened relations between the USSR and USA
Soviet invasion of Afghanistan		
'Evil empire' speech		
Strategic Defence Initiative		

2 Explain why relations between the USA and the USSR worsened in the years 1979–85.

Exam tip: q2 This is a Unit 1 style question. You will need to:
● identify at least three reasons
● make links between each of these reasons
● prioritise the reasons. In other words, explain which you think was the most important and why.

6.3 President Gorbachev and the end of the Cold War

In March 1985, Mikhail Gorbachev became leader of the Soviet Union and immediately set about reforming the old Soviet system and improving relations with the USA.

Internal reforms

Gorbachev was the decisive figure in this period. He firmly believed that the USSR could not continue to compete with the USA and that the Soviet Union needed to be reformed. The twin themes of his policies were:

● *Perestroika* – changing some economic policies to allow more competition and more incentives to produce goods. Gorbachev wanted to change the government-controlled economy that had been in place since the time of Stalin.
● *Glasnost* – openness in government. Gorbachev thought people should be allowed, within reason, to say what they believe with more open debate.

Ending the Cold War

Gorbachev was able to improve relations with the USA and end the Cold War.

Weaknesses of the USSR

Gorbachev realised that the Soviet Union could not continue the Cold War.
● It was committed to an expensive war in Afghanistan.
● The economy could not sustain increased defence spending.
● The USA seemed to have forged ahead in space and computer technology.
● The USA had also forged ahead in the arms race with the development of SDI.
● There was growing discontent in the **satellite states** of eastern Europe against Communism and Soviet control. One example of this was the Solidarity trade union movement in Poland which achieved much support in the early 1980s.

Gorbachev and Reagan

The two leaders met on several occasions and got on well together.
● Gorbachev accepted Reagan's invitation to meet with him in Geneva in November 1985. The two leaders were able to talk face-to-face although there was no formal agreement on arms limitations.
● The two met again at Reykjavik in October 1986. Again there was no formal agreement because Reagan refused to drop the SDI project.
● SALT had developed into START (Strategic Arms Reduction Talks) and, on an official visit to Washington in December 1988, Gorbachev also proposed deep cuts in conventional (non-nuclear) American and Soviet forces.

Comment

These new policies led to many practical changes within the USSR. Some political prisoners were released – for example, Andrei Sakharov, a nuclear physicist-turned-human rights campaigner, was allowed to return from exile. In 1987, changes in economic policy meant that people were allowed to buy and sell at a profit for the first time since the 1920s.

Key terms

Satellite state: a country under the influence or control of another state.

INF treaty

In 1987, after several meetings, Gorbachev and Reagan signed the Intermediate-range Nuclear Forces (INF) treaty, which removed all medium-range nuclear weapons from Europe. Gorbachev signed the treaty because:

- he believed that this would increase his popularity in the West
- the Soviet economy could not recover due to the amount being spent on nuclear weapons
- Reagan told Gorbachev that he had no intention of invading the USSR.

The break-up of eastern Europe

During 1989, Gorbachev was at the height of his international popularity. He met the new American president, George Bush, and together they announced the end of the Cold War. In 1990, he was awarded the Nobel Peace Prize. Yet in 1989, Soviet control of eastern Europe was collapsing rapidly.

The eastern bloc

The Communist countries of eastern Europe had become increasingly discontented during the 1980s. It gradually became clear that the Soviet Union had neither the will nor the power to put down demonstrations or prevent changes in these nations' systems of government. Even so, the speed of the collapse of Soviet control amazed everyone.

- Poland: free elections were held in June 1989. Lech Walesa became the first non-Communist leader in eastern Europe since 1945.
- East Germany: the unpopular East German leader, Erich Honecker, tried to prevent change, but his troops refused to fire on the demonstrators. In November 1989 the Berlin Wall was pulled down.
- Czechoslovakia: in November 1989 there were huge anti-Communist demonstrations. Vaclav Havel, a popular playwright, became the new leader of the country, with free elections in 1990.
- Romania: in a short and bloody revolution in December 1989 the unpopular Communist dictator Nicolae Ceauşescu and his wife Elena were shot.
- Bulgaria: the Communist leader resigned in November 1989 and free elections were held in 1990.
- The Baltic states: in 1990 Lithuania, Latvia and Estonia declared themselves independent of the Soviet Union.

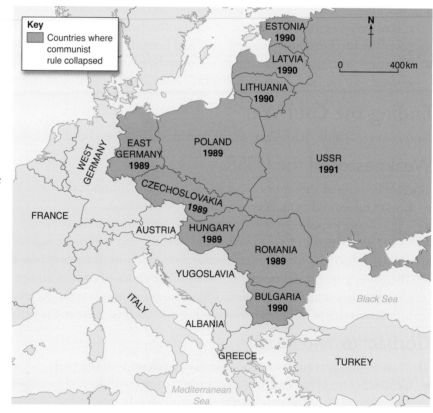

The collapse of Communism in eastern Europe.

The fall of the Berlin Wall

The fall of the Berlin Wall came to symbolise the end of the Cold War. On 9 November 1989 the East German Government announced much greater freedom of travel for East German citizens, including crossing the border into West Germany. Thousands of East Berliners flocked to the checkpoints in the Berlin Wall and the border guards let them pass. Soon, the East Berliners were chipping away at and dismantling the wall.

The fall of the Soviet Union

Gorbachev was seen as weak by many within the Soviet Union. His promised reforms had not brought about improved living standards and he appeared to have simply allowed the collapse of Soviet influence in eastern Europe. Some in the USSR itself did not want the mere reform of Communism, but its abolition.

In 1991, East and West Berlin were reunited, and East and West Germany became a single country. In other ex-Communist countries there were less happy endings. For example, in Yugoslavia the Serbs refused to accept a Croat as leader, and Slovenia and Croatia declared independence in 1991, leading to a bloody civil war. The era of Communism in eastern Europe was over.

Revision tasks

1 Draw a mind map to explain briefly the part played by the following in the collapse of the USSR:
   - *Perestroika*
   - *Glasnost*
   - Boris Yeltsin.

2 Why was Gorbachev so liked and so hated at the same time?

3 Make a copy of the table below and summarise the key developments in each country in the years 1989–90.

Poland	
Czechoslovakia	
East Germany	
Romania	
Bulgaria	
Hungary	
The Baltic states	

Key content

You need to have a good working knowledge of the following areas:

- the meaning of Détente and its key features
- the reasons for and impact of the Soviet invasion of Afghanistan
- the reaction of President Carter
- the Second Cold War, the 'evil empire' and SDI
- the policies of President Gorbachev
- the end of the Cold War, including the summits between Reagan and Gorbachev and the INF Treaty
- the break-up of eastern Europe, including the fall of the Berlin Wall
- the break-up of the Soviet Union and the fall of Gorbachev.

In 1918 Germany was defeated in the First World War. The country was in chaos and there were attempts at revolution. In the 1920s Germany recovered, but the Depression caused enormous problems which allowed Hitler and the Nazi Party to gain power. Hitler's Third Reich brought benefits to certain groups in Germany in the period 1933 to 1939, but proved disastrous for others.

Key issues

As with all examination topics, you will be expected to do more than simply learn the content and write it out again. You will need to show understanding of key issues from the period. These are:

- the Weimar Republic, 1918–33
- Hitler and the growth of the Nazi Party, 1918–33
- the Nazi dictatorship, 1933–39
- Nazi domestic policies, 1933–39.

7.1 The Weimar Republic, 1918–33

The **Weimar Republic**, which was set up after the First World War, faced a number of problems in its early years. It experienced a period of recovery in the years 1924–29, only to be badly affected by the Great Depression.

The origins of the Weimar Republic, 1918–23

Defeat in the First World War led to the **abdication** of **Kaiser** Wilhelm II and the establishment of a new republic.

There was revolution in Germany in October–November 1918 due to the effects of the First World War:

- The British navy had imposed a naval blockade of German ports which left Germany short of food and essential supplies. The winter of 1917–18 was nicknamed the 'turnip winter' because of the dependence on turnips as a source of food.
- The British, French and US armies had driven the German troops out of France and Belgium and were close to the German borders.
- A flu epidemic was sweeping the country, killing thousands of people already weakened by rations.

The revolution began with sailors in the port of Kiel who, at the end of October 1918, refused to go to sea and instead marched on Berlin. This triggered other revolts. On 9 November the Kaiser abdicated and on the following day a republic was set up under **Chancellor** Ebert. On 11 November the new republic signed the **armistice** with the Allies.

The early problems of the Weimar Republic, 1919–23

Ebert and his colleagues drew up a new democratic **constitution** for Germany and, in the summer of 1919, Ebert was elected its first President.

> ## Key terms
>
> **Weimar Republic:** a republic is a country without a hereditary ruler, such as a king or emperor. The new Government first met in the town of Weimar.
> **Abdication:** to give up the throne.
> **Kaiser:** emperor.
> **Chancellor:** chief minister (equivalent of Prime Minister in Britain).
> **Armistice:** a ceasefire.
> **Constitution:** an agreed method of governing a country, with the details usually written down and agreed on by those being governed.

A democratic Germany

In theory, the new Weimar constitution gave Germany a nearly perfect democratic system.

- The 'lower house', or Reichstag, was elected by **proportional representation**. The vote was by secret ballot and universal suffrage (everyone could vote). Elections were to be held at least every four years.
- The 'upper house', or Reichsrat, was made up of representatives from each of the German states. It could delay new laws.
- The President was also the head of state and was elected every seven years. The President appointed the Chancellor (usually the head of the largest party in the Reichstag) to form a government. The Chancellor's role was therefore similar to the Prime Minister's role in Britain.

In practice, it proved very difficult to get one party into power (see below).

Weaknesses of the new constitution

- In 1919, the Republic had many enemies. Was it sensible to give equal rights to those who wished to destroy it?
- Proportional representation encouraged lots of small parties. It was difficult for one party to get a majority so governments had to be **coalitions** where two or more parties joined together. This led to weak governments.
- The President had too much power. Article 48 of the constitution said that in an emergency, the President could abandon democracy and rule by decree. This proved disastrous in the period 1929–33.
- The army generals were the same men who had fought the war for the Kaiser. Many of them opposed the Republic and wanted the Kaiser to return.
- The judges in the new Germany were the same men who had served under the Kaiser. They had sympathy with those who were against the Republic.

Effects of the Treaty of Versailles

See Chapter 2 for the effects of the Treaty of Versailles on Germany.

The German Government had no choice but to sign the treaty, but this had several unfortunate results.

- The new Republic got off to a bad start and was immediately associated with the humiliating treaty.
- Opponents of the Republic, especially the army, blamed the Government for signing the armistice that led to the treaty. They referred to the Government as the 'November Criminals'; a reference to the signing of the armistice on 11 November.
- The Government was accused of having stabbed the German army in the back. In other words, the German army would have won the war if the armistice had not been signed. This, of course, was not true.
- Germany could not afford to pay the reparations. The country had been run down by the war and had lost important areas of land which could make money, such as the coalfields of the Saar.

Exam tip You will need to know the weaknesses of the German constitution, especially the effects of proportional representation and Article 48.

Exam tip Be aware of the terms of the Treaty of Versailles, how they affected Germany and why they brought widespread opposition.

Revision tasks

1 Draw up a balance sheet of strengths and weaknesses of the new Weimar constitution by writing key words in a table like this:

Strengths	Weaknesses

2 Describe the events which led to the setting up of the Weimar Republic.

Exam tip: q2 This is an example of a question from Unit 2. You need to describe at least two factors.

3 Re-read Chapter 2. Make a copy of the following table. Complete it to show reasons for German discontent with the Treaty of Versailles.

Military terms	
War guilt	
Rhineland	
Reparations	
Loss of land	

Opposition from the left – the Spartacists

Communists in Germany, known as Spartacists, wanted a revolution similar to that in Russia in 1917 (see page 75).

- In January 1919, Communist activists led by Karl Liebknecht and Rosa Luxemburg seized power in Berlin and the Baltic ports.
- In Bavaria, an independent socialist state was created under the leadership of Kurt Eisner.
- Within weeks, however, all the revolts had been crushed by regular troops and ex-soldiers (Freikorps). The Communist leaders were assassinated.

Opposition from the right – the Kapp Putsch

German **nationalists** thought democracy was weak. For many nationalists, the new Weimar Republic was a symbol of Germany's defeat in the war. They were furious with the Government for signing the Treaty of Versailles. They wanted to see a strong government that would make Germany great once again.

- In March 1920, Wolfgang Kapp, an extreme nationalist, and a group of Freikorps units seized power in Berlin. This became known as the Kapp **Putsch**.
- Kapp was not supported by the workers in the factories. The workers organised a strike in Berlin in support of the Government. Within hours, the German capital came to a halt and supplies of gas, water and coal stopped.
- After four days, Kapp and his supporters gave up and fled Berlin. Ebert and the Weimar Government returned to power.

The French occupation of the Ruhr

According to the terms of the Treaty of Versailles, Germany had to pay for the damage caused during the First World War. These payments were known as reparations and were a major burden to the new state.

- The Reparations Commission announced that Germany would be required to pay £6,600 million in gold in annual instalments.
- In 1922, the German Government announced it would not be able to pay and asked for more time.

The British Government agreed to this but the French Government insisted that Germany must pay. In January 1923, the French and Belgian Governments sent troops into the Ruhr, the centre of German industry. The results were disastrous for Germany.

- German workers used **passive resistance** against the invaders and refused to work.
- The German economy ground to a halt.

Hyperinflation

The problem of making the reparation payments encouraged the Weimar Government to print more and more money. However, printing money simply caused prices to rise out of control and hyperinflation set in. The German mark became virtually worthless.

- As prices rose, people's savings became worthless (this hit the middle classes particularly hard). In 1923, prices in shops were increased almost every hour.
- At times, workers were paid twice a day so that they might be able to buy food before prices rose again.
- People on fixed incomes (such as pensioners) suffered badly.
- Prices rose much faster than incomes and many people starved as they were unable to afford food or fuel.

Value of the German mark against the US dollar, 1914–23	
1914	$1 = 4 marks
1922	$1 = 7,000 marks
July 1923	$1 = 160,000 marks
November 1923	$1 = 4,200,000,000 marks

Revision tasks

1 Make a copy of the table below. Use the information in this section to write a key word summary of each event and give each a rating on a scale of 1 to 10 in terms of its seriousness for the Weimar Republic.

Threat	Date	Outline of events	Rating
Spartacist revolt			
Kapp Putsch			
French invasion of the Ruhr			
Hyperinflation			

2 Explain why the Weimar Republic faced attacks from the left and right in the years 1919–23.

3 Who or what were the following?
- Spartacists
- Kapp
- Article 48
- the Rentenmark

Exam tip: q2 This is a Unit 2 question. You will need to:
- fully explain at least two reasons
- make links between each reason
- prioritise the reasons. Which do you think was the most important reason and why?

The recovery of the Republic under Stresemann, 1924–29

The role of Stresemann

As Chancellor, Stresemann tried to stabilise Germany's financial position, as shown in the previous section. Stresemann became Foreign Secretary in 1924 and was mainly responsible for the Dawes Plan and German success abroad. He died in October 1929, on the eve of the Wall Street Crash. He was one of the few Weimar politicians strong enough to appeal to the German people.

Economic recovery

This was encouraged by the introduction of:
- the Rentenmark, which replaced the old worthless mark
- the Dawes Plan of 1924 – in return for Germany starting to pay reparations once more, the USA agreed to lend Germany 800 million marks. This could be used to build new factories to produce jobs and goods, and to raise people's standard of living.

During this period, the Weimar Republic seemed to recover from the problems of its early years. This is often referred to as the 'Golden Age' of the Republic. The success was due to several reasons.

- In 1925, the French and Belgian troops left the Ruhr.
- In 1928, industrial production finally improved on pre-First World War levels. By 1930, Germany was one of the leading exporters of manufactured goods.
- In 1929, the Young Plan was introduced, which reduced reparations by over 67 per cent.
- In nearly every town, new factories and public facilities sprang up. New roads, railways, and nearly three million homes were built.

Political stability

The period 1924–29 saw more stable governments. After the 1928 election, the Social Democrats, for the first time since 1923, joined a government coalition with the other parties that supported the Republic. This showed that the middle-class parties were no longer so suspicious of the socialists. There was less support for extreme parties such as the National Socialist German Workers' Party (the Nazis), who won only twelve seats in the Reichstag in the elections of 1928. The Communists also did less well in 1924 and 1928.

Foreign policy

Stresemann was responsible for several successes in foreign policy.

- In 1925 Germany signed the Locarno Treaties with Britain, France and Italy. These guaranteed Germany's frontiers with France and Belgium.
- In 1926 Stresemann took Germany into the League of Nations. Germany was recognised as a great power and was given a permanent seat on the League's Council alongside France and Britain.
- In 1928 Germany signed the Kellogg–Briand Pact along with 64 other nations. It was agreed that they would keep their armies for self-defence but 'the solution of all disputes shall only be sought by peaceful means'.

Problems

However, there were still serious problems.

- Germany depended on American loans, which could be withdrawn at any time.
- Farming suffered from depression throughout the 1920s due to a fall in food prices. Income from agriculture went down from 1925 to 1929.
- Extremist parties such as the Nazis and the Communists were determined to overthrow the Weimar Republic. In 1924 the Communists held 45 seats in the Reichstag and this grew to 54 seats in the 1928 election.
- In 1925 Hindenburg was elected President. He had been one of Germany's war leaders under the Kaiser and disliked the new Republic.

The impact of the Great Depression, 1929–33

The period of recovery under Stresemann ended in 1929 with the Wall Street Crash.

Effects of the Wall Street Crash, 1929

The recovery of the German economy was fragile. It depended heavily on American loans. In 1929, disaster struck with the Wall Street Crash.

- Many American banks were forced to recall their loans. German companies were unable to pay.
- German businesses began to close. Millions lost their jobs.

Unemployment and the rise of extremism

From 1928 to 1930, German unemployment rose from 2.5 million to 4 million. This was an opportunity for extremist groups such as the Communists and the Nazis.

- As unemployment rose, more and more people felt let down by the Weimar Government and began to support extremist parties.
- In the 1930 election, the Communists increased their number of seats in the Reichstag from 54 to 77.
- Nazi support increased from 12 seats in 1928 to 107 in 1930. The Nazis were now the second largest political party in the Reichstag.

Revision task

1 How had Germany changed in the years 1923–29 as a result of Stresemann's policies? Use a key word list to summarise the changes in the following table.

	1923	1929
The economy		
Political situation		
Foreign policy		

2 Draw a timeline of the Weimar Republic from 1919–30. On your timeline:
   a) add the key developments
   b) shade in red those developments which weakened or threatened the Republic
   c) shade in green those which strengthened it.

7.2 Hitler and the growth of the Nazi Party, 1918–33

The Nazi Party, which was one of the most important extremist groups, was able to take advantage of the problems experienced by the Weimar Republic in the years 1929–32.

The early Nazi Party

Hitler's career before 1919

Hitler was born in Austria in 1889. At the age of sixteen he left school and went to Vienna to pursue his ambition of becoming a painter. This did not work out and between 1909 and 1914 he was virtually destitute, living on the streets of Vienna. It was during these years that he developed his hatred of the Jews:

- **Anti-Semitism** was widespread in Vienna.
- He was envious of the wealthy Jews and blamed them for his own problems.

When war broke out in 1914 Hitler joined the German army and served with distinction, winning the Iron Cross. He found it hard to accept the armistice, believing Germany was on the verge of winning the war when it was betrayed by the politicians. Hitler stayed in the army after the war, working in Munich for the intelligence services. It was in this job that he came across the German Workers' Party led by Anton Drexler.

The Nazi Party, 1919–23

In 1919, Hitler joined the German Workers' Party.

- He changed its name to the National Socialist German Workers' Party (Nazis) and took over as leader in 1921.

Key terms

Anti-Semitism: hatred of Jews.

Exam tip You will need to be aware of how Hitler's early career shaped his views of the Jews and the Weimar Republic and led him to a career in politics.

- He organised his own private army called the Sturm Abteilung (SA), or Stormtroopers, who were used to protect Nazi meetings and attack those of their opponents, especially the Communists.
- Hitler drew up a 25-point programme, which included the promise to reverse the terms of the Treaty of Versailles, destroy Communism and make Germany great. It also included an attack on the Jews, blaming them for Germany's defeat in the First World War.
- He attracted support from extreme nationalists and by 1922 the Nazi Party had 3,000 members.

The Munich Putsch and the lean years

In 1923 Hitler made his first attempt to seize power.

The Munich Putsch, 1923

In November 1923, Hitler and the Nazis tried to seize control of the Bavarian Government. The plan was to capture Munich and from there march on Berlin. Hitler was convinced people would join him in overthrowing the failed Weimar regime.

Hitler had several reasons for carrying out the Putsch:
- The Weimar Republic was very unpopular due to the French occupation of the Ruhr and hyperinflation.
- In 1922 the Italian leader, Benito Mussolini, had seized power after a march on Rome.
- Hitler was convinced that he would get popular support in Munich.

The attempt is sometimes called the Beer Hall Putsch because of where it began.
- On 8 November, Hitler forced members of the Bavarian Government to join him, at gunpoint. Its leader, Gustav Von Kahr, was reluctant to do so and alerted the army and the police.
- The Nazi plan soon began to go wrong. The next day, Bavarian police opened fire on Nazi Stormtroopers in Munich and sixteen Nazis were killed.
- Hitler and Ludendorff (the former First World War general who was now a Nazi supporter) were arrested and charged with high treason.

However, it was clear that Hitler's views had some support in Germany.
- Hitler received the minimum sentence. Many Nazi supporters also received light sentences.
- Hitler served his sentence in the comfortable Landsberg Fortress and spent his time writing his memoirs.
- The memoirs were later published as *Mein Kampf* (*My Struggle*). In this book, Hitler outlined his view of German history and his views on Germany's rightful place in the world.

> **Exam tip** If asked about the effects of the Munich Putsch on Hitler and the Nazi Party, remember to give a balanced view. It was a short-term failure but brought more long-term benefits to the party.

The lean years, 1924–29

This was a period of mixed fortunes for the Nazi Party. On the one hand, the Nazi Party did not do well.
- It won only twelve seats in the election of 1928.
- There were quarrels and disagreements within the party during Hitler's period in prison.

On the other hand, there was progress.
- Hitler had learnt from the mistake of the Munich Putsch and was determined to achieve power through legal methods – by securing a majority of seats in the Reichstag.
- He reorganised the party to make it more efficient, setting up a headquarters in Munich and branches of the party all over Germany.

Revision tasks

1 How did Hitler change the Nazi Party in the period 1919–23?

2 Make a copy of the table below. Use key words to explain the causes, events and results of the Munich Putsch.

	The Munich Putsch
Causes	
Events	
Results	

3 Make a copy of this set of scales. Write in the pans key words about the development of the Nazi Party, 1923–29, including the effects of the Munich Putsch.

4 Do you think the Nazi Party was stronger or weaker in 1929, compared to 1923?

Weaker

Stronger

Increased support, 1929–33

The Great Depression of 1929 onwards transformed the fortunes of the Nazi Party.

How the Depression helped Hitler

The Depression helped Hitler in several ways.

- It caused a period of chaos in Germany.
- No government could take control of the situation and solve Germany's terrible economic problems.
- Unemployment was the big issue. By January 1932, it stood at six million. Hitler promised to get these people back to work. Through clever campaigning and his brilliant speaking skills, Hitler gained support in many parts of German society, including that of wealthy and powerful industrialists. Josef Goebbels was responsible for the Nazi propaganda and election campaigns. He realised the attraction of Hitler's speeches and used air travel to move Hitler quickly from place to place.
- There were frequent street battles between the Communists (Hitler's greatest rivals) and the police. In contrast, the SA gave an impression of discipline and order. Many people felt that the country needed this type of order.

In two years, Hitler led the Nazi Party from being the second largest party in the Reichstag to being the only legal party in Germany. By July 1933, the Weimar Republic and the democracy it represented had been destroyed.

The events of 1932–January 1933

In July 1932 there was a general election which triggered great violence. Nazis and Communists fought each other in street battles and nearly 100 people were killed.

The Nazis became the largest party in the Reichstag and Hitler demanded to be made Chancellor. However, Hindenburg was suspicious of Hitler and refused. Instead, he appointed Franz von Papen, a conservative politician with no party base, as Chancellor.

To achieve his aims, von Papen needed to increase his support in the Reichstag and so he called another election in November 1932. The Nazis lost seats but were still the largest party. Von Papen did not get the extra support he needed.

It was becoming increasingly clear that President Hindenburg could not continue to work with a Chancellor who did not have support in the Reichstag. Von Papen simply could not pass any of the measures he wanted.

In December 1932 Hindenburg replaced von Papen with Kurt von Schleicher, one of his advisers. Within a month, however, von Schleicher was forced to resign.

- Hindenburg and von Papen decided to make Hitler Chancellor.
- They believed they would be able to control him once he was in power.
- On 30 January 1933, Hitler became German Chancellor and von Papen became Vice-Chancellor.

Exam tip The events of 1932 are very complex. However, you will need a thorough knowledge of what took place, especially the roles of Hindenburg and von Papen.

Revision tasks

1 What factors changed the prospects for the Nazis between the beginning and end of the 1920s? Use four to six key words for your answer.

2 Draw a flow chart to show the key events of 1932–33 which brought Hitler to power.

3 Do you think that President Hindenburg underestimated Hitler?

4 Put the following events in chronological order:
- the Munich Putsch
- Hitler joins the German Workers' Party
- Hitler is invited to become Chancellor
- the Nazis become the largest party in the Reichstag
- Hitler is in prison
- Hitler introduces the 25-point programme

7.3 The Nazi dictatorship, 1933–39

In the years 1933–39 Hitler established a dictatorship of the Nazi Party.

The removal of opposition, 1933–34

As soon as he was appointed Chancellor, Hitler tried to find a way of raising the number of Nazis in his government. He persuaded Hindenburg to dissolve the Reichstag and to hold another general election.

The Reichstag fire, February 1933

During the election campaign, on the night of 27 February 1933, the Reichstag was burnt to the ground. A Communist, Marinus van der Lubbe, was arrested for the crime. Hitler and the Nazis were able to exploit the fire for their own purposes.

- The Nazis were quick to blame the Communist Party.
- Hitler persuaded President Hindenburg to pass an emergency law restricting personal liberty.
- Using the law, thousands of Communist supporters were thrown into prison.

Despite increasing their share of the vote in the election, the Nazis still did not have an overall majority in the Reichstag. They were forced to join together with the 52 nationalist members to create a government.

The Enabling Act, March 1933

Hitler still did not have enough support to have complete control of Germany. An Enabling Act would give him the right to pass laws for the next four years without having to obtain the support of members in the Reichstag. However, to pass an Enabling Act Hitler needed to obtain the votes of two-thirds of Reichstag members, but he had the support of only just over half. This is what happened.

- Hitler ordered his SA to continue intimidating the opposition.
- The 81 Communist members of the Reichstag were expelled.
- In an atmosphere heavy with violence and threats, the Enabling Act was passed by 441 votes to 94.

- Hitler was given the power to rule for four years without consulting the Reichstag.

In July 1933, Hitler increased his grip on power even further. Using the powers of the Enabling Act, he outlawed all other parties and Germany became a one-party state. The democratic Weimar Republic had been destroyed and Germany had become a dictatorship.

Then Hitler turned on the trade unions.

- On 2 May 1933, Nazis broke into trade union offices all over the country and arrested thousands of trade union officials.
- Unions were banned and all workers became part of the German Labour Front.

The Night of the Long Knives

Once he had gained power, Hitler's priority was to rid himself of possible rivals. Ernst Röhm, leader of the SA, had played a major role in helping Hitler achieve power. However:

- The German army saw the SA as a rival – the army would not support Hitler unless the SA was disbanded.
- Some members of the SA looked to Hitler to follow a socialist programme of reform – Hitler was opposed to this since he knew he would lose the support of wealthy industrialists.
- Röhm was a threat to Hitler's dominance of the Nazi Party.

Hitler made a deal with the generals of the German army. They promised to support him as commander-in-chief of the armed forces if the SA was disbanded, and if he started a programme of rearmament. On 30 June 1934, SS assassination squads murdered Hitler's potential SA rivals, including Röhm (the SS was set up in 1925 as an elite section of the SA). It has been estimated that up to 400 people were killed in the 'Night of the Long Knives'.

Just over one month later, President Hindenburg died. Hitler thereafter combined the posts of Chancellor and President and also became commander-in-chief of the armed forces. From this point onwards, soldiers swore personal allegiance to Hitler, who officially became known as *der Führer* (the leader).

Revision task

Make a copy of the following table. Use key words to complete each column to show how Hitler achieved his dictatorship.

	What Hitler did	Importance
Reichstag fire		
The Enabling Act		
The SA		

The police state

In July 1933, Germany became a one-party state. All other political parties were banned and people who openly criticised the Nazis were imprisoned – or worse. This policy was enforced ruthlessly by the SS (Hitler's bodyguard) and the Gestapo (secret police).

- They used terror tactics to intimidate, arrest and even kill any possible opponents.
- Enemies of the Nazis, such as liberals, socialists and Communists, were often arrested and sent to concentration camps without trial.

Nazi control of society

The Nazis took control of key areas of everyday life.

Law courts

The legal system was controlled by the Nazis.
- There was no trial by jury.
- All judges were Nazis.

The Churches

The Catholic and Protestant Churches were seen as a threat because Christianity was very different from the beliefs of Nazism.
- A Nazi Reich Church was set up to replace the Protestant Church.
- The Catholic Church was persecuted and priests were arrested.

Censorship and propaganda

The Nazis believed in complete loyalty and obedience. One of the main tools used to achieve this was propaganda. Hitler made Josef Goebbels Minister of Enlightenment and Propaganda. Goebbels' job was to spread Nazi ideas and encourage all Germans to be loyal to Hitler. Goebbels (a former journalist) used his new power to control all information that reached the German people.
- All newspapers were censored by the Government and allowed to print only stories favourable to the Nazis.
- Radio was controlled by the Government. Cheap radios were manufactured so that most Germans could afford one. Goebbels made sure that all radio plays, stories and news items were favourable to the Nazis.
- The Nazis took control of the German film industry. German films of the 1930s often showed great German heroes defeating their enemies. Cartoons were used to show Jews as weak and devious.
- Goebbels organised mass rallies. The most spectacular was held each August in Nuremberg. At the rallies, hundreds of thousands of Nazi supporters listened to choirs, sang songs and watched sporting events and firework displays.
- The Nazis used sporting events to spread their propaganda. The 1936 Berlin Olympic Games was used by the Nazis to suggest the superiority of the 'Aryan race'. ('Aryan' was the Nazi term for non-Jewish Germans.)

7.4 Nazi domestic policies, 1933–39

Nazi policies brought many changes for the young, women, the unemployed and Jews.

Nazi policies towards the young and women

The Nazis had their own views about the role of the young and women.

Young people

Education was targeted:
- Teachers had to swear an oath of loyalty to Hitler and join the Nazi Teachers' League. Teachers had to promote Nazi ideals in the classroom.
- The curriculum was changed to prepare students for their future roles. Hitler wanted healthy, fit men and women so fifteen per cent of time was devoted to physical education. With the boys the educational emphasis was on preparation for the military. Girls took needlework and home crafts, especially cookery, to become good homemakers and mothers.
- New subjects such as race studies were introduced to put across Nazi ideas on race and population control.

Exam tip Remember that Nazi control was based on fear, through the police state, and persuasion, through censorship and propaganda.

Revision tasks

1 Draw a mind map to show all the different methods used by the Nazis to control the German people – this should include the police state, censorship and propaganda.

2 Describe the key features of the police state under the Nazis.

Exam tip: q2 This is an example of a question from Unit 2. You need to describe at least two factors.

- Textbooks were rewritten to fit the Nazi view of history and racial purity. Hitler's *Mein Kampf* became a standard text.

The Nazis also wanted to control the young in their spare time. This was achieved through the Hitler Youth.
- All other youth organisations were banned and from 1936 membership of the Hitler Youth was compulsory. By 1939 there were 7 million members.
- Boys joined the German Young People at the age of ten. From fourteen to eighteen they became members of the Hitler Youth. They learned Nazi songs and ideas and took part in athletics, hiking and camping. As they got older they practised marching, map reading and military skills. Many enjoyed the comradeship.
- Girls joined the Young Girls at the age of ten. From fourteen to eighteen they joined the League of German Maidens. They did much the same as the boys, except they also learned domestic skills in preparation for motherhood and marriage and there was much less emphasis on military training.

Women

The Nazis believed in the traditional domestic role of women, which was to marry, have children and look after the home. This was summarised as the 'three Ks': *Kinder, Küche, Kirche* – children, kitchen, church.

The Nazis brought in the following changes:
- They reduced the number of women, especially married women, in employment. However, due to rearmament, more women were employed in industry after 1937.
- Hitler wanted to increase the birth rate and encouraged German women to marry and have as many children as possible. Married couples were given loans based on the number of children they had.
- They believed in the traditional natural appearance of women, with long hair, no make-up and long skirts. Women were discouraged from smoking and drinking.

Revision tasks

1 Make a copy of the following table. Use key words to summarise the changes brought in by the Nazis for young people and women in the years 1933–39.

	Schooling		Youth movements
Young people			
	Appearance	Employment	Marriage
Women			

2 Explain the changes brought in by the Nazis to the position and role of women in Germany in the years 1933–39.

Exam tip: q2 This is a Unit 2 question. You will need to:
- fully explain at least two changes
- try to make links between each change
- prioritise the changes. Which do you think was the most important and why?

Employment and the standard of living

Employment

Hitler had promised to remove unemployment. This was achieved by 1938 through a variety of policies.
- The Labour Service Corps was set up. From 1935, it was compulsory for all men aged 18–25 to serve in the Corps for six months.
- Unemployed men were put to work building government-funded roads, motorways, houses, hospitals and schools.
- From 1935, all men aged 18–25 were compelled to do military service for two years.

- Rearmament provided thousands of jobs in arms factories and greatly boosted heavy industry.

The standard of living

There is much debate about whether the German people were better or worse off under the Nazis in the years 1933–39.

Better off	Worse off
<ul><li>There was more or less full employment.</li><li>The 'Strength Through Joy' movement organised leisure activities and provided the public with sports facilities, cheap holidays and entertainments. It also helped to plan the production of a 'people's car' (Volkswagen) that was cheap enough for many workers to afford. Many new motorways (autobahns) were built in the 1930s by the unemployed.</li><li>'Beauty with Labour' was a department of 'Strength Through Joy' and tried to improve working conditions by organising the building of canteens and sports facilities for workers.</li></ul>	<ul><li>The Labour Front replaced trade unions. Workers were not allowed to leave their jobs without government permission, and strikes were made illegal. Opposition was rare. By the late 1930s, pay had increased and workers accepted the long working hours and lack of rights because of higher pay.</li><li>The Volkswagen scheme was a swindle. People were encouraged to save five marks per week to buy their own car. By the time war broke out in 1939 not a single customer had taken delivery of a car. Moreover, the money was never refunded.</li><li>The Nazis used dubious methods to keep down the unemployment figures. The figures did not show 'invisible unemployment' which included Jews and married women forced to leave their jobs.</li></ul>

The persecution of minorities

The Nazis believed in the superiority of the Aryan race (non-Jewish Germans). They persecuted members of other races, and many minority groups such as Gypsies, homosexuals and mentally and physically disabled people. They persecuted any group that they thought challenged Nazi ideas.

- Gypsies were thought to be an inferior people. Five out of six Gypsies living in Germany in 1939 were killed by the Nazis.

The treatment of Jews

Although all groups who posed a threat to the Nazi regime were persecuted, it was the Jews who received the worst treatment of all.

In 1933, the Nazis organised a boycott of all Jewish businesses, doctors, dentists, and so on. Jewish shops were marked with the Star of David and the word '*Jude*' (Jew). In education, Jewish children were intimidated at school and Germans were taught that Jews were unclean and responsible for Germany's defeat in the First World War.

In 1935 the Nuremberg Laws were introduced in Germany. Under these laws:

- Jews could no longer be German citizens
- marriages between Jews and Aryans were forbidden
- Jews had to wear a yellow star on their clothing.

Kristallnacht

It is not clear how much most Germans knew about the persecution. However, in 1938 an event occurred that left nobody in any doubt.

In early November 1938, a Polish Jew, Herschel Grynszpan, shot a German diplomat in Paris. Hitler ordered an immediate attack on Jews and their property in Germany. Between 9 and 10 November, thousands of Jewish businesses were attacked and 200 synagogues burnt down. This was called *Kristallnacht*, 'The Night of Broken Glass'. Violence against Jews in Germany increased. Himmler, head of the SS, began to plan the expansion of concentration camps.

Revision tasks

1 Do you think that workers were better or worse off under the Nazis? Give reasons for your answer.

2

SOURCE 1

From a history of Germany published in 2007.

Röhm wanted to incorporate the army into the SA and was also hoping for reforms to help the workers. He was disappointed with Hitler's close relations with army leaders and industrialists. In addition, Himmler, the leader of the SS, Hitler's personal bodyguard, wished to break away from the SA and the control of Röhm.

What can you learn from Source 1 about the reasons for the Night of the Long Knives?

3 Make a copy of the following table and use the information in this section to complete it.

Minority group	Why Nazis persecuted them	How they were persecuted
Jews		
Gypsies		

Exam tip: q2 This is a Unit 2 inference question. That means you have to identify at least one inference or message and back it up with evidence from the source. Begin your answer with 'This source suggests …'.

Key content

You need to have a good working knowledge of the following areas:

- the origins of the Weimar Republic, especially the revolution of November 1918
- the early problems of the Weimar Republic, including the weaknesses of the new constitution, the Treaty of Versailles and attacks from the left and right
- the French occupation of the Ruhr and hyperinflation
- the recovery of the Republic under Stresemann in the years 1924–29
- the impact of the Great Depression on Germany, 1929–33
- Hitler's early career and the setting up of the Nazi Party
- the early development of the Nazi Party, 1920–23
- the causes, events and results of the Munich Putsch of 1923
- the changes in the Nazi Party 1924–29 and the growth in support after 1929
- the events of 1932–33 which brought Hitler to power
- the removal of opposition 1933–34, including the Reichstag fire, the Enabling Act and the Night of the Long Knives
- control of the Churches and the German people through the police state and propaganda
- changes in the position of women, the young and the unemployed
- Nazi policies towards the Jews in the years 1933–39.

Chapter 8: Russia, 1917–39

In 1914, Russia was ruled by Tsar Nicholas II and went to war against Germany and Austria. The war was a disaster, with defeat after defeat and economic, political and military chaos. In 1917, there were two revolutions. These were followed by three years of civil war. The Communists emerged triumphant under Lenin, who introduced a series of reforms designed to modernise the country. Stalin won the leadership contest that followed Lenin's death and introduced a series of reforms in agriculture and industry in an attempt to modernise the Soviet economy.

Key issues

As with all examination topics, you will be expected to do more than simply learn the content and write it out again. You will need to show understanding of key issues from the period. These are:
- the collapse of the Tsarist regime, 1917
- Bolshevik takeover and consolidation, 1917–24
- the nature of Stalin's dictatorship, 1924–39
- economic and social changes, 1928–39.

8.1 The collapse of the Tsarist regime, 1917

In March 1917 Tsar Nicholas II abdicated due to the growth of opposition and the impact of the First World War.

The nature of Tsarist rule

There was much opposition to Tsarist rule in the years before 1917.

The Tsarist system of government

The Russian monarch was known as the Tsar. He ruled as an **autocrat**. He believed that God had made him Tsar and that he therefore had absolute authority to rule Russia. The Tsar ruled with the support of the aristocracy (landowners), the Church, the army and the civil service.

Discontent

Various groups had become discontented before and during the First World War:
- The peasants, who formed 80 per cent of the population, often lived in extreme poverty and wanted to own their land.
- Industrial workers in large cities such as Petrograd and Moscow lived in overcrowded conditions and worked long hours for very little pay.
- **Subject nationalities** such as Poles, Lithuanians and Finns were being forced to speak the Russian language and accept Russian customs. They wanted their independence.

The growth of opposition

There were several groups opposing the Tsar.

- The Social Revolutionaries were the largest and most violent group and were supported by the peasants. They wanted to carve up the huge estates of the very rich and hand them over to the peasants.
- The Bolsheviks were a small group of dedicated revolutionaries led by Lenin who wanted to overthrow the Tsar and set up a Communist government.
- The Mensheviks wanted to create a mass Communist party which would eventually overthrow the Tsar.
- The Constitutional Democrats or Cadets wanted to keep the Tsar but make him share power with a parliament or **Duma**.

The impact of the First World War

In 1914 Russia went to war on the side of Britain and France and against Germany and Austria–Hungary. The war had disastrous effects for the Tsar.

Political chaos

While dealing with the war, the Tsar left the Government of Russia in the hands of his wife Alexandra. This created problems:

- Alexandra was unpopular because of her German background.
- Until his assassination in December 1916, she was under the influence of a monk called Rasputin.
- Alexandra dismissed capable ministers and refused to accept the advice of the Duma.
- She misled the Tsar about the extent of opposition in Petrograd.

Military defeat

Continued military defeat increased the unpopularity of the Tsar. The Russian soldiers were often poorly equipped due to shortages of weapons and ammunition. They suffered a series of crushing defeats at the hands of the Germans, including the Battle of Tannenburg in August 1914. They were further weakened by the long-term effects of the Brusilov offensive of 1916, which resulted in one million casualties and further hardship at home.

The Tsar took personal command of the army in 1915. This was a mistake as he was then held directly to blame for any defeats.

Economic chaos

The Russian economy could not cope with the increased demands of war.

- There was even greater overcrowding in the towns and cities, as well as low wages and rising prices.
- The Russian transport system proved totally inadequate and food often failed to reach towns and cities.
- There were serious fuel shortages by the end of 1916.

Social misery

By the end of 1916 there was discontent throughout Russia.

- In the towns and cities there were high prices and food and fuel shortages.
- In the countryside there were too few peasants to work on the land due to conscription. Consequently they suffered from increasing food shortages.
- Conditions in the army were so bad (with a lack of equipment and even boots) that an increasing number of soldiers deserted.
- There was a severe winter (even by Russian standards) in 1916–17.

Revision tasks

1 Draw a mind map showing the effects of the First World War on Russia. On your mind map draw lines to show links between each effect. Use key words along the line to explain each link.

2 Explain the effects of the First World War on Russia by the beginning of 1917.

Exam tip: q2 This is a Unit 2 question. You will need to:
- fully explain at least two effects
- try to make links between each effect
- prioritise the effects. Which do you think was the most important and why?

The fall of the Tsar

The effects of the First World War led to the February Revolution. The unrest began in February 1917 with a strike at the Puetilov steelworks in Petrograd.
- Unrest and strikes spread quickly and bread queues turned into riots.
- The workers began to form councils (called Soviets) and the leaders of the Duma (including Alexander Kerensky – see below) began to oppose the Tsar openly.
- By the end of February the troops had joined the rioters and the Tsar had no choice but to abdicate (give up power) on 3 March. The Tsar's regime was replaced by a provisional government.

Comment

This is often called the March Revolution because in 1917 Russia was using a different calendar from the West. As a result, the first Russian revolution took place in February by the Russian calendar, but March for the rest of Europe. This book will use the 'Russian' dates.

The Provisional Government

After the abdication of the Tsar in 1917, the Duma appointed a Provisional Government headed at first by Prince Lvov. He was replaced by Alexander Kerensky in July of that year. Kerensky had already served in the Provisional Government as Justice Minister and War Minister. He was also Deputy Chairman of the Petrograd Soviet (worker's council). Many people already believed that the soviets were more effective as a means of government than the Duma.

Lenin and Bolsheviks

At the time of the February Revolution, Lenin, the leader of the Bolsheviks, was in exile in Germany. On his return, a month after the abdication of the Tsar, his aim was to overthrow the Provisional Government with a second revolution of the working classes.

Lenin published his views in April 1917 in the 'April Theses'. In simple terms, he said that the Bolsheviks offered 'peace, land and bread, all the power to the soviets'.

The Kornilov revolt

Alexander Kerensky began to take a grip on his opponents and Lenin was forced to leave Russia again. However, Kerensky was then challenged by the new commander of the army, General Kornilov, who wanted to impose a strict regime and crush opponents, rather like the Tsar had done.

Kerensky asked the Bolsheviks to help him defeat Kornilov, which they did. Kerensky was now in real trouble. He had lost the support of the army and was dependent upon the Petrograd Soviet (with its strong Bolshevik influence) to run Russia.

Mistakes made by the Provisional Government

The Provisional Government made several mistakes which weakened its position.
- It continued the war effort out of loyalty to Russia's allies and in return for supplies. The offensive of June 1917 was a disastrous failure and was followed by further German advances and more desertions for the Russian armed forces.
- Failure to end the war worsened the food shortages in the towns and cities.
- Because of its temporary nature, the Provisional Government would not carry out important reforms. For example, it failed to give land to the peasants, which increased discontent in the countryside.

- The Provisional Government allowed opposition parties, including Lenin and the Bolsheviks, to campaign in Russia. Real authority and support lay with the Petrograd Soviet.

Revision tasks

1 Make a copy of the following table. Use the information in this section to explain how each of the following weakened the Provisional Government.

	How weakened
Petrograd Soviet	
Lenin	
Kornilov revolt	

2 Describe the key features of the Provisional Government.

Exam tip: q2 This is an example of a question from Unit 2. You need to describe at least two factors.

8.2 Bolshevik takeover and consolidation, 1917–24

The second revolution of 1917 led to a Bolshevik takeover and three years of civil war.

The October Revolution

In October 1917 the Provisional Government was overthrown.

The Bolshevik takeover

Bolshevik support increased throughout 1917.
- In September the Bolsheviks became the largest party in the Petrograd Soviet. They also controlled the Military Committee of the Soviet, with Leon Trotsky becoming chairman.
- Trotsky used the Military Committee to plan the revolution.
- On 16 October Lenin returned to Russia (he had been forced into hiding abroad in July) and was now convinced that the time was right to overthrow the Provisional Government.
- On 24 and 25 October the Bolsheviks seized power. They took control of the key locations of Petrograd and Moscow, including the Post Office, bridges, State Bank and railway stations.
- Red Guards stormed the Winter Palace and arrested the ministers of the Provisional Government. Kerensky managed to escape and tried to rally loyal troops. When this failed, he fled into exile.

Reasons for Bolshevik success

Bolshevik success was due to various reasons.
- The Provisional Government was very unpopular. Few rallied to support Kerensky and there were no massive demonstrations demanding his return.
- Lenin played an important role. He had spent many years organising a disciplined party dedicated to revolution. His campaigning of 1917, especially his slogan 'Peace, Land and Bread', brought more support. By October, the Bolshevik Party had 800,000 members with supporters in strategic places. At least half the army supported it, as did the sailors at the important naval base at Kronstadt, near Petrograd. The major industrial centres, and the Petrograd and Moscow soviets, were also pro-Bolshevik.
- The October Revolution is often described as a classic work of planning by Trotsky. He organised the seizure of key buildings and positions in the two major cities.

Exam tip Many students confuse the two revolutions of 1917. Remember the first was spontaneous opposition which led to the abdication of the Tsar. The second was a planned takeover by a group of revolutionaries.

Imposing Bolshevik control, 1918–21

It took the Bolsheviks three years to establish control of Russia.

The Constituent Assembly

Lenin was not interested in democracy. The elections that were held late in 1917 showed that the Bolsheviks did not have the support of most Russians.

- The Constituent Assembly, which met in January 1918, contained twice as many Socialist Revolutionaries (SRs) as Bolsheviks, and the SRs opposed Lenin.
- Bolshevik Red Guards closed down the Assembly. By July 1918, the Russian Congress of Soviets had agreed a new system of government for Russia.

The result was that Lenin effectively became a dictator, and his secret police (the Cheka) began to intimidate, imprison and murder political opponents.

The Treaty of Brest-Litovsk

The Bolsheviks had always planned to pull out of the war with Germany. They agreed a ceasefire in December 1917. Trotsky was given the job of negotiating terms but his only real achievement was to hold up the Germans until March 1918, when the Bolsheviks were forced to sign the Treaty of Brest-Litovsk.

- Russia lost vast amounts of territory (see map below).
- Russia lost important coal and iron resources and about one-third of its population.
- Russia also had to pay 300 million gold roubles in compensation.

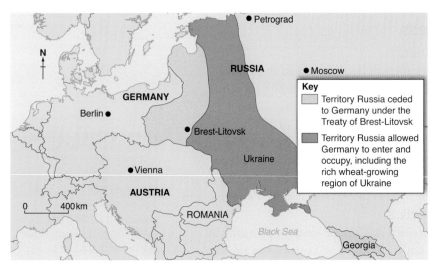

Russian losses under the Treaty of Brest-Litovsk.

The Civil War, 1918–22

The Bolsheviks had to fight a war against a number of opponents.

Who made up the opposition?

The Bolsheviks did not have the support of all Russians when they seized power. By May 1918, they had more enemies, especially after the losses of the Treaty of Brest-Litovsk. By the summer of 1918, the Bolsheviks were faced with a range of opponents united only by their opposition to the Bolsheviks. These opponents, called the Whites (in contrast to the Bolshevik Red Guards), were made up of former tsarists, Mensheviks, Socialist Revolutionaries and foreign powers opposed to the new regime in Russia.

The Bolsheviks in danger

In the early stages of the Civil War, the Bolsheviks faced several different threats.

- The Czech legion (which was made up of former prisoners of war) had seized sections of the vital Trans-Siberian railway.
- Admiral Kolchak had set up a White government in Siberia and was marching on Moscow.
- General Denikin was advancing with his army from southern Russia.
- Northern Russia, led by General Yudenich, was opposing the Bolsheviks.
- There were also risings against the Bolsheviks in Ukraine and Turkestan.
- Foreign powers supplied the Whites with arms and weapons and later landed troops to help the Whites. American, Japanese, French and British troops landed at Archangel, Murmansk and Vladivostok.

Bolshevik victory

Against what seemed to be overwhelming odds, the Bolsheviks won the Civil War. The crucial year was 1919. Under Trotsky's leadership, the Red Army defeated Kolchak and destroyed the Czech legion. Denikin's advance on Moscow was stopped and by 1920 he was being pushed back. By late 1920, White forces were completely defeated. The Bolsheviks had won due to their ruthless, disciplined commitment and the failings of their enemies.

The strengths of the Bolsheviks were:

- they had large, well-organised armies under Trotsky, and good communications
- they made good use of propaganda to show that the Whites were in league with foreigners and wanted to bring back the Tsar
- together with the Cheka (secret police), they kept a ruthless control over the Bolshevik territories, making sure that most people obeyed Lenin's rule
- the Red Army was supplied by the brutal policy of 'War Communism' (see page 78), which ensured that troops and towns were fed and supplied
- they controlled major towns with factories and industries to support the war effort.

The failings of the Whites were:

- they had no aim upon which they all agreed – in some cases, they disliked each other almost as much as they opposed the Bolsheviks
- their forces were spread across a huge area and they could not co-ordinate their attacks – they were beaten one by one
- their harsh treatment of people in the lands they captured led many to support the Bolsheviks against them.

1 Make a copy of the following table about the reasons for the Bolshevik victory in the Civil War. Use the information in this section to complete it.

Bolshevik strengths	White weaknesses

2 Explain why the Bolsheviks defeated the Whites in the Civil War of 1918–21.

Exam tip: q2 This is a Unit 2 question. You will need to:
- fully explain at least two reasons
- make links between each reason
- prioritise the reasons. Which do you think was the most important and why?

Creating a new society, 1918–24

The Bolsheviks introduced two very different economic policies: War Communism and the New Economic Policy.

War Communism

To defeat his opponents in the civil war, Lenin knew that he had to make sure that his armies were fed and equipped. To achieve this, he introduced the policy of '**War Communism**'.

- Land and industry were 'nationalised' – taken over by the state.
- In the factories there was severe discipline (for example, strikers could be shot) and key items such as food and coal were rationed.
- In the countryside, peasants were forced to hand over their surplus produce (what they did not need themselves) to the Government.
- Opposition was rooted out and destroyed by the Cheka (even the royal family was executed).

> **Key terms**
>
> **War Communism:** had the *appearance* of Communism, but was being carried out due to Bolshevik necessities during the Civil War.

The cost of the Civil War and War Communism

By 1921 Lenin was facing a shattered and demoralised country.

- War Communism had made the industrial workers poor and restless.
- War Communism and war damage had led to famine in the countryside – millions died in 1921.

The Kronstadt mutiny of 1921 was a turning point. The Kronstadt sailors had been leading supporters of the revolution, but they revolted against War Communism in February 1921.

Although the Kronstadt revolt was put down by Trotsky and the Civil War was being won, it was clear in 1921 that Lenin had to do something to improve people's living conditions. His solution was to replace War Communism with the New Economic Policy (NEP).

The New Economic Policy

Lenin introduced the NEP at the Bolshevik Party Congress in March 1921. Its measures were simple but controversial.

- Peasants could keep part of their surpluses to sell at a profit.
- Small factories were given back to private ownership.
- Small private businesses could be set up to trade at a profit.

Some Communists saw the NEP as a betrayal, but Lenin saw it as a temporary measure to keep the Russian people happy and get the economy moving. All of the major industries remained in state hands, and political control (under the Cheka) remained very strict.

Exam tip Do not confuse the two economic policies. Remember that the NEP was a temporary move back to capitalism.

Revision tasks

1 Make a copy of the following table. Use key words to show the difference between War Communism and the NEP.

	Aims	Key features	Effects
War Communism			
NEP			

2 Place the following events in chronological order:
- Introduction of NEP
- Kronstadt mutiny
- Treaty of Brest-Litovsk
- The end of War Communism
- Constituent Assembly

8.3 The nature of Stalin's dictatorship, 1924–39

Stalin eventually succeeded Lenin as leader of the USSR and ruthlessly removed his rivals to establish a dictatorship.

The struggle for power, 1924–28

There was a leadership contest following the death of Lenin.

The candidates

There were two main rivals:
- **Trotsky**. When Lenin died, Trotsky was the most obvious candidate to take over the leadership of the Communists. He was brilliant, talented and had an outstanding 'track record' as leader of the Bolshevik Army.
- **Stalin**. Stalin expressed no strong views – he was a hard working administrator and few expected him to win the leadership contest.

Reasons for Stalin's success

The leadership contest was eventually won by Stalin, although it took him five years to become completely established as Lenin's successor. Stalin was able to defeat his rivals for a number of reasons.
- He had taken on many important jobs (editor of the party newspaper *Pravda*, Commissar for Nationalities, Secretary-General of the party). This gave him an important power base – he had many supporters in the ranks of the party (who owed their positions to him).
- Stalin took advantage of the **Lenin Enrolment** to increase his support within the party. He also appeared as the chief mourner at Lenin's funeral while tricking Trotsky into missing it.
- Trotsky made himself unpopular. His ideas for spreading world revolution alarmed moderate Communists. He was also arrogant and offended many party members.

The purges of the 1930s

Stalin used the purges to remove all possible opposition.

Reasons

In 1934, Stalin's ally Sergei Kirov was murdered. Stalin saw this as evidence of a conspiracy and began a series of political purges (involving imprisonment and execution). Historians are now fairly sure that Stalin planned Kirov's murder to give him an excuse to purge the USSR of opponents, whom Stalin saw as traitors to himself and the USSR.

Key Terms

Lenin Enrolment: a process started in 1923, lasting until 1925, to try to get more industrial workers in the Communist Party.

Revision task

Draw a mind map showing the reasons why Stalin was successful in the leadership contest. Put the reasons on order, clockwise, beginning with the most important at twelve o'clock.

Key features

From 1934 to 1938, thousands were arrested, imprisoned, murdered or simply disappeared. They came from all areas of Soviet life.

- The Communist Party: the number of party members fell from 3.5 million in 1934 to two million in 1935.
- Leading party members such as Zinoviev, Kamenev and Bukharin were tortured and their families threatened. Then, at show trials, they 'confessed' and were executed.
- Many less important opponents (and even supporters who were not enthusiastic enough) were arrested and either executed or sent to labour camps (*gulags*).
- In 1937, around 25,000 army officers (including the Commander of the Red Army, Marshal Tukhachevsky) were purged.

Show trials

These began in 1936 when Stalin began purging the Communist Party of anyone who might oppose him, especially the 'Old Bolsheviks' such as Kamenev and Zinoviev. The accused were put on trial in full view of the world and forced to confess to a whole range of unlikely crimes. The confessions were important because they appeared to show that Stalin was right to carry out the purges.

Effects

The effects of the purges were mixed. Stalin was certainly secure. His new secret police (the NKVD) ruled the population with terror. Over 8 million people had been killed or sent to labour camps. However, Stalin had weakened the USSR. Many of those purged had been skilled or educated (for example, managers or army officers) and so industrial progress slowed down. The army was seriously weakened and suffered badly against the Germans in 1941.

Propaganda and censorship

Propaganda was also used to build up hero-worship of their leader. This was known as the cult of Stalin.

- The Soviet people were flooded with portraits, photographs and statues of Stalin. Every town had a Stalin Square, a Stalin Avenue or a Stalin statue in the centre.
- Poets and playwrights praised Stalin, whilst regular processions were organised through the streets of Russian towns and cities praising Stalin's achievements.
- History was re-written to show Stalin as a close friend of Lenin and a key figure in the Bolshevik revolution.

Education

In 1932 a rigid programme of education was introduced in which children were taught that Stalin was the 'Great Leader' as well as Stalin's version of history. The teaching of Communist ideology became compulsory in schools, whilst education focused on technical and scientific skills which were needed by workers involved in the Five-Year Plans (see page 82).

The constitution

Stalin made himself more secure still in 1936 with the USSR's new constitution. At first sight, it appeared more democratic – all citizens voted for members of the **Supreme Soviet**. However, it had no real power and decisions were still made by Stalin and his closest supporters.

Exam tip Students often have a sound knowledge of the purges. However, they are less secure in their knowledge of propaganda and the cult of Stalin.

Key terms

Supreme Soviet: an elected body of representatives (the equivalent of the British Parliament), but which had no real power. It only met for two weeks a year. It was the Communist Party under Stalin that made the important decisions.

Economic and social changes, 1928–39

Stalin believed that the USSR was under threat from non-Communist states. He also believed that the only way to make the country secure was for it to become a modern, industrial nation. His aim was to force the USSR to make fifty years' progress in ten years. There were two key aspects of Stalin's plans:
- the need to improve food production (collectivisation)
- the need to expand heavy industry (Five-Year Plans).

Collectivisation

Stalin brought in major changes to the countryside in the USSR.

Reasons

Stalin had made clear his ambitions to transform the USSR. The Five-Year Plans could work only if Soviet agriculture could raise its production massively. There were two main reasons for doing this.
- To feed the growing population of industrial workers.
- To export any surpluses to raise cash for investment in industry.

Key features

Most farms were smallholdings tended by peasant families. These holdings could never be efficient enough for Stalin's plans so he introduced the policy of collectivisation.
- Peasants effectively had to give up their land and join other families on very large farms.
- These new farms were supplied by the state with seed, tools, tractors and other machinery.
- Most of the produce went to the Government.

The real opponents of collectivisation were the kulaks. Kulaks were peasants who had become prosperous under the NEP, and they made up a large and important part of the population of the countryside. Most refused to co-operate with the new policy because they did not want to give up their land.

Effects

The effects of collectivisation were very mixed, but this policy certainly had less of a claim to success than the Five-Year Plans (see page 82). This is what happened.
- By 1941, almost all land in the USSR was collectivised.
- A huge propaganda campaign was launched to convince peasants to modernise.
- Kulaks were murdered or put in labour camps – many killed their own animals or burned their crops rather than let the Government have them.
- Much of the countryside was devastated by struggles between Stalin's agents and the kulaks.

- Although collectivisation was achieved, food production fell dramatically. In the Ukraine, there was famine in the early 1930s and at the same time food was being exported.

The long-term result of this struggle was that the peasants were battered into submission and never again seriously threatened the Communist regime.

Industrialisation

In 1928 Stalin introduced the first of his Five-Year Plans.

The Five-Year Plans

Stalin seemed to have several clear reasons for industrialising the USSR. These were:
- security
- to create a showpiece of success for the outside world
- to carry out his idea of 'socialism in one country'.

In order to achieve his aims, he came up with two Five-Year Plans for the development of the USSR. They presented incredibly ambitious targets for industrial production that had to be achieved in five years.

Although few targets were met (see right), the industries that failed to meet their targets still made huge advances.

Effects

Historians disagree about the aims and effects of the Five-Year Plans. One thing on which all historians agree is that the USSR was transformed.
- The main aim was achieved – by 1940, the USSR was in the 'first division' of industrial powers, along with Britain, Germany and the USA.
- Vast projects such as the Belomor Canal, the Dnieper Dam and the metalworks at Magnitogorsk were completed with amazing speed.
- Huge towns and factories were built from nothing, deep inside the USSR to protect them from invasion.
- Foreign technicians were brought in and enormous investment was put into education and training to produce skilled workers.
- Great pressure was put on workers to meet targets and to be 'Stakhanovites'. Stakhanov was a miner who managed to produce over 100 tonnes of coal in one shift, and was held up as a model to inspire all workers.
- The cost was high. Safety standards came second to meeting targets, discipline was harsh and many workers ended up in labour camps. All investment went into heavy industries – there were few consumer goods (clothes, luxuries).
- However, by the mid-1930s there were definite signs of improved living standards (for example, education, welfare, housing).

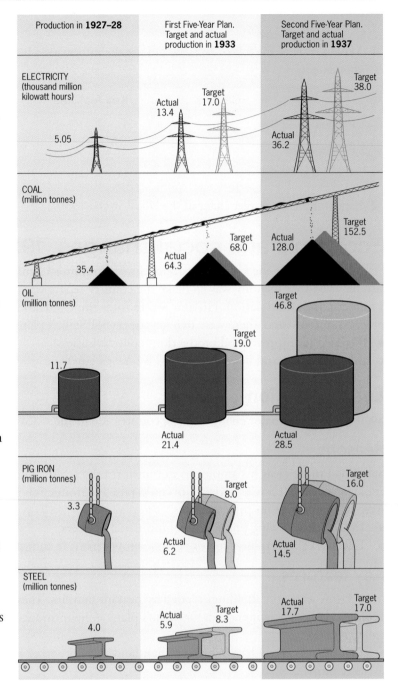

Target and actual production under the first two Five-Year Plans.

Exam tip If you are asked a question about industrialisation do not write about collectivisation except if you think it affected the Five-Year Plans.

Life in the Soviet Union

Everyday life was transformed in the years 1928–39.

Living conditions and working conditions

- For the mass of the peasantry life was worse than that of town workers. The state kept prices low to ensure a cheap supply of food for the towns. As a result, more and more peasants moved to the towns to find work and, hopefully, a better standard of living.
- Some workers were promoted into management jobs in industry. For example, over one and a half million workers gained management posts under the first Five-Year Plan.
- Some workers also benefited from the expansion of higher education which enabled them to gain the technical knowledge needed for higher management posts.
- In addition, the rapid industrialisation caused by the Five-Year Plans removed any areas of unemployment.
- The down side was that the urban population rose from 29 million in 1929 to 40 million only four years later. This, in turn, led to poor living conditions. Furthermore, working conditions were harsh with strict rules about discipline and punctuality.
- As peasants flooded into towns and cities, all the basic amenities became overcrowded. Trams and buses were jam packed. Flats had to be shared by several families. Often, there was one family per room and they had to share the bathroom and kitchen. In Moscow, only six per cent of families lived in more than one room.

Women

- Women made progress in the area of employment. They were encouraged to work in almost all areas. Some women took on jobs like engineering, which had once been done only by men. However, life remained hard for most Soviet women. They were expected to work full time, as well as bring up a family. Help was provided by state nurseries and crèches.
- Politically, women still remained second-class citizens, with less than twenty per cent of the Communist Party membership being women and very few women rising to high positions in the party or government.

Ethnic minorities

Although Stalin was from an ethnic minority group within the Soviet Union, the Georgians, he had no sympathy for the plight of these non-Russian groups and gave them a hard time. He wanted to turn them into 'Soviet citizens' rather than, for example, Ukrainians or Georgians.

- Minority groups were discouraged from speaking their own languages and practising their own customs and traditions.
- They were often discriminated against with few gaining high positions in industry or the armed forces.
- They were targets of Stalin's purges. From 1935 the Soviet Government carried out 'cleansing' operations in border regions. Finnish, Latvian and Estonian families were deported from the Leningrad region to Kazakhstan and Siberia.

Revision tasks

1 Draw a mind map on one side of A3 paper to show the changes that Stalin brought to the USSR in the years 1928–39. Include the purges, propaganda, the cult of Stalin, industrialisation, collectivisation, living and working conditions and the role of women.

2

SOURCE 1

From a history of Russia and the USSR published in 2006.

Lenin and Trotsky played crucial roles in the Bolshevik takeover. Trotsky was the organiser, carefully planning the revolution. Lenin showed tremendous vitality and enthusiasm and gave the Bolsheviks simple slogans which were easily understood by the Russian people. He was able to exploit the mistakes of the Provisional Government.

What can you learn from Source 1 about the reasons for the success of the Bolshevik takeover in October 1917?

Exam tip: q2 This is a Unit 2 inference question. That means you have to identify at least one inference or message and back it up with evidence from the source. Begin your answer with 'This source suggests ...'.

Key content

You need to have a good working knowledge of the following areas:

- the nature of Tsarist rule and the growth of opposition groups
- the impact of the First World War on Russia, especially military defeat and economic and social effects
- the key features of the February Revolution of 1917
- the mistakes and weaknesses of the Provisional Government
- the reasons for the success of the Bolshevik takeover
- the key features of Lenin's government, especially the Treaty of Brest-Litovsk and the Constituent Assembly
- the reasons for Bolshevik success in the Civil War
- the key features of War Communism and the NEP
- how and why Stalin succeeded Lenin as leader
- how Stalin established his dictatorship, especially the purges and propaganda
- the reasons for, key features of and effects of collectivisation and industrialisation
- the changes in living and working conditions and the role of women.

After the First World War, people in Europe looked to the USA for leadership – both to help prevent future wars and for financial assistance to help rebuild Europe's shattered economies. But the Americans had problems of their own.

Key issues

As with all examination topics, you will be expected to do more than simply learn the content and write it out again. You will need to show understanding of key issues from the period. These are:

- the US economy, 1919–29
- US society, 1919–29
- the USA in depression, 1929–33
- Roosevelt and the New Deal, 1933–41.

9.1 The US economy, 1919–29

In the 1920s the US economy experienced a period of growth, although not all industries shared in this boom.

Causes and consequences of the economic boom

The boom was due to several factors.

The US economy before 1920

In the early years of the First World War, American businesses profited from the war in Europe.

- American industries supplied arms and equipment.
- American firms were able to take over much of the export business of the European powers while they were caught up in the fighting.

The First World War made the USA wealthy and confident. Americans felt they were doing well. It also made them isolationist. They did not want to be dragged into Europe's wars.

Republican policies

Throughout the 1920s, Republican presidents were in power, and they implemented Republican policies. President Harding's key policies were isolation, tariffs and low taxes to help businesses to grow, and to give workers money to spend. When Harding died suddenly in 1923, Vice-President Coolidge continued to follow the same policies.

The boom period

In the 1920s, the profits of many American companies rose enormously. More goods were produced more quickly and more cheaply because of new mass-production techniques. The biggest boom came in the industries making consumer goods – goods for ordinary families to buy. Sales of household goods such as vacuum cleaners and washing machines boosted the electrical industry.

The single most important industry was the motor industry. Cars were becoming increasingly common and by 1930 there were 30 million on the roads of the USA. A healthy car industry helped create further jobs in related areas, such as car parts and road building.

Another factor in the boom was the use of labour-saving devices in American factories. Modern techniques, especially the assembly line, simplified jobs and resulted in dramatic increases in production. Advertising, credit and hire purchase made it easy to spend. Wages for many Americans rose, and there was a feeling of confidence in the economy.

As well as buying goods, ordinary Americans wanted a share of some of the profits which companies were making. To do this, they bought and sold shares in companies.

Revision tasks

1 Make a copy of these concentric circles. Write a reason for the boom in each circle, beginning with the most important in the middle. Explain your decisions.

2 Explain why the USA experienced an economic boom in the 1920s.

Exam tip: q2 This is a Unit 2 question. You will need to:
- fully explain at least two reasons
- make links between each reason
- prioritise the reasons. Which do you think was the most important and why?

Declining industries

Despite the boom there were still many Americans living in poverty. Workers in many older industries did not benefit from the economic growth.

Coal industry

The demand for coal declined due to competition from new forms of power such as gas and electricity. There were wage cuts and job losses. In 1928 there was a strike in the coal industry in North Carolina, where the workers were paid only $18 for a 70-hour week when $48 per week was considered the minimum required for a decent life.

Cotton industry

This industry also suffered from competition due to the development of new man-made fibres such as rayon. Again there were job losses and wage cuts.

Problems in agriculture

Agriculture suffered a serious decline in the 1920s. Some reasons were:
- After the First World War Europe imported far less food from the USA.
- Farmers were also struggling against competition from highly efficient Canadian wheat producers.
- There was overproduction in farming due to improved mechanisation, especially the introduction of the combine harvester. By 1920 farmers were producing surpluses that nobody wanted.

Prices fell as desperate farmers tried to sell their produce. In 1921 prices fell by 50 per cent. Many farmers were ruined. There were five times as many rural bankruptcies in the 1920s than in the twenty years previous.

6 million rural Americans, mainly farm labourers, were forced off the land in the 1920s. Many of these were unskilled workers who moved to the cities.

Exam tip Candidates often have very good knowledge of the growth industries in the boom. However you also need to know about the declining old industries and the problems in agriculture.

Revision tasks

1 Use four to six words to explain the problems of the older industries in the 1920s.

2 Make a copy of the following table. Use the information in this section to complete it.

	Reasons	Effects
Problems in agriculture		

9.2 US society, 1919–29

Like its economy, American society was full of contrasts in the 1920s. There were very real advances for some Americans – they owned cars and electrical goods, and enjoyed themselves as never before.

The 'Roaring Twenties'

This was the name given to life in the USA in the 1920s.

Consumerism

The economic boom of the 1920s was partly encouraged by the growth of consumerism. This meant the growing demand for everyday, often household, goods by many Americans. Increased demand for consumer goods was due to several factors:

- By 1927 two-thirds of US homes had electricity. This stimulated the demand for electrical goods such as washing machines and vacuum cleaners. The growth in female employment (see below) also increased the need for these labour-saving devices.
- Hire purchase schemes made it easier to buy goods on credit.
- The popularity of entertainment meant more and more Americans bought radios.
- For the majority of workers in industry, wages increased. Between 1923 and 1929 the average wage rose by eight per cent. In other words, workers had more spare money to spend on consumer goods.

Entertainment

During the 1920s, films became a national obsession. Millions of Americans went to the cinema each week to watch new stars such as Buster Keaton and Charlie Chaplin. Hollywood became the centre of a multi-million dollar industry.

The 'Jazz Age'

The 1920s is known as the 'Jazz Age' because the popular music of the time was jazz. The writer F. Scott Fitzgerald coined the phrase in 1922 in his book *The Beautiful and The Damned*.

Jazz was not new. It originated with African American slaves who were encouraged to sing in order to increase production. They used washboards, cans, pickaxes and percussion to produce their own distinctive brand of music. Their music was given various names including 'blues', 'rag' or 'boogie-woogie'. By changing the beat and creating particular rhythms, it was changed into jazz.

Women

After the First World War, women were given the vote in the USA. At this time, they gained greater freedom by working and earning their own money. One symbol of this new independence was the flappers – independent young women named after their short skirts. They cut their hair short, wore make-up and smoke and drank in public. They also openly danced with men in public (especially the new craze, the Charleston), listened to jazz and drove cars and motorbikes.

Revision tasks

1 In fewer than five words, define:
- the 'Roaring Twenties'
- the 'Jazz Age'
- a flapper.

2 Describe the key features of the 'Roaring Twenties'.

However, although about eight million women were now working, mainly as teachers or secretaries, more women were housewives doing the work they had always done.

Prohibition and gangsters

One of the most controversial features of the USA in the 1920s was the effect of prohibition.

Prohibition

By the end of the First World War, there was a strong temperance (anti-alcohol) movement in the USA. Temperance groups pressured the Government to pass the Eighteenth Amendment to the US Constitution – prohibition. Brewing or selling alcohol was now illegal in the USA.

Prohibition was essentially a failure. It didn't stop the alcohol trade – it simply drove it underground. **Bootleggers** made large amounts of money smuggling alcohol into the USA, or through illegal brewing. Secret bars, called speakeasies, were easy to find if people wanted a drink. Even the American President was known to drink.

Gangsters

Gangs of criminals began to run bootlegging and other forms of crime (gambling, drugs, prostitution) almost like a business. These gangs would sometimes fight with each other for control of the trade.

The most notorious gang leader was Al Capone, who virtually controlled the city of Chicago by bribing the mayor and other politicians. Capone was almost certainly responsible for the St Valentine's Day Massacre in 1929 when six members of a rival gang were killed.

Racism and intolerance

At the same time as some young Americans were experiencing liberation, others were facing intolerance and racism.

The Red Scare

The Communist revolution in Russia (see Chapter 7) alarmed some Americans, particularly leading industrialists. They saw the USA's trade unions as a threat which could lead to revolution.

The **radicals** in the USA's immigrant communities were immediate targets. They were suspected of planning revolution. Police, soldiers and ex-servicemen disrupted meetings and raided offices, and thousands of people were arrested. The Government was involved in, and supported, this campaign.

It was nothing like the scale of what was to come in Nazi Germany, but this was an unpleasant aspect of the USA in the 1920s. In one extreme case, two Italian radicals, Sacco and Vanzetti, were executed for murder. Most historians are now convinced that they were innocent of this crime (see below).

The Sacco and Vanzetti case

Sacco and Vanzetti were Italian immigrants. They were known anarchists who hated the American system of government. In 1920, they were charged with the murder of two guards during an armed robbery.

Exam tip: q2 This is an example of a question from Unit 2. You need to describe at least two factors.

Revision task

Explain how prohibition changed US society in the 1920s.

Exam tip This is a Unit 2 question. You will need to:
- fully explain at least two changes
- make links between the changes
- prioritise the changes. Which do you think was the most important and why?

Key terms

Bootleggers: people who carried liquor into the USA from Canada or Mexico. The name comes from the fact that they sometimes hid the bottles inside their knee-length boots.

Radicals: people or groups (sometimes within other groups) who hold extreme political views.

- Sixty-one eyewitnesses identified them as the killers.
- The defence found 107 witnesses who swore to seeing the men elsewhere. These were mostly Italian immigrants.
- The two men were found guilty and executed in 1927.
- In 1977, the verdict against the men was declared unjust because the judge presiding over the case had been prejudiced against the men's political views.

The Monkey Trial

Most people living in the towns and cities of the USA accepted Charles Darwin's theory of evolution, which suggested that over a period of millions of years human beings had evolved from ape-like creatures. However, these views were not accepted by many people in rural areas, especially in the so-called '**Bible Belt**' states such as Tennessee. Many in these areas were known as fundamentalists. They held strong Protestant Christian beliefs, including the belief that the Biblical account of God creating humans on the sixth day was literally true.

Six US states chose to ban the teaching of Darwin's theory of evolution in their schools. A biology teacher called John Scopes decided to challenge this ban. He deliberately taught evolution in his class in Tennessee in order to be arrested and put on trial. Scopes was convicted of breaking the law. However, the trial was a disaster for the public image of the fundamentalists. Their leader, William Jennings Bryan, was shown to be confused and ignorant whilst the media mocked the beliefs of those who opposed the theory of evolution.

Racism

Forty-one of the white-controlled state governments, fearing the power of African Americans, introduced laws to control the freedom of African American people in the years after 1865. These were known as the **Jim Crow** laws. The state government **segregated** African American people from white people in schools, parks, hospitals, swimming pools, libraries and other public places. After the First World War new Jim Crow laws were passed in some states so that there were segregated taxis, race tracks and boxing matches.

The Ku Klux Klan

The Klan was another example of the darker side of the 1920s in the USA. It was originally formed to terrorise African American slaves after they had been given freedom in the nineteenth century. As well as African Americans, the Klan also attacked Catholics and Jews. It was a movement of mainly poor whites concerned about their livelihoods in 1920s USA.

Key terms

Bible Belt: those states in America where Protestant fundamentalism is strong.
Jim Crow: a name made popular by a white American comedian who made fun of African Americans. Originally, Jim Crow was a character in an old song. This name became linked to the southern laws ensuring that African American people remained inferior.
Segregation: keeping a group separate from the rest of society, usually on the basis of race or religion. Segregation was seen in separate schools, transport and housing.

Revision task

Make a copy of the following table.
a) In column 2, use key words to summarise each example of racism and intolerance in the USA in the 1920s.
b) In column 3, give each example a rating out of 5 to show how serious it was, with 5 being the most serious.

	Key features	How serious (1–5)
The Ku Klux Klan		
Sacco and Vanzetti		
The Monkey Trial		
The Red Scare		

9.3 The USA in depression, 1929–33

The boom of the 1920s came to a sudden end with the Wall Street Crash of 1929 which was followed by the Great Depression.

Causes and consequences of the Wall Street Crash

The Wall Street Crash was a result of long-term weaknesses in the US economy and the short-term problems of the stock market.

Weaknesses in the US economy

There were worrying weaknesses in the American economy during the period building up to the Crash.

- Some major industries did not grow in the 1920s (for example coal and textiles).
- Farmers had produced too much food and prices were very low.
- Many ordinary Americans did not share in the boom. African Americans, in particular, suffered from discrimination, getting the worst jobs.
- Some industries were struggling against foreign competition.
- Other industries could not export goods because of tariffs in other countries. Often these tariffs were simply a reaction to American tariffs already in place.

Short-term causes of the Crash

Short-term causes related to shares. Many ordinary Americans bought shares in companies. Normally this is good for business. However, in the USA in the 1920s the rush to buy shares caused problems.

- Many people bought and sold shares to make quick profits instead of keeping their money invested in the same businesses for some time. They were speculators, not investors.
- Companies were forced by shareholders to pay out profits to shareholders rather than reinvesting the profits.
- Americans borrowed money on credit to buy their shares.

These kind of share dealings depended on confidence that share prices would continue to rise. Once people started worrying about the long-term weaknesses in the American economy, disaster struck. In September 1929, the prices of shares began to edge down – slowly to start with – but people soon began to realise that the shares they owned were worth less than the loans they had used to buy them in the first place. All of a sudden, everyone tried to get rid of their shares, selling them for less and less. The worst day was 'Black Tuesday', 29 October 1929. As a result, share prices collapsed.

The immediate effects

The effects of the Crash were disastrous.

- Many individuals were bankrupt – they could not pay back the loans they used to buy their (now worthless) shares.
- Some homeowners lost their homes as they could not pay their mortgages.
- Even some of those who had savings lost their money when banks collapsed.
- Many farmers suffered a similar fate as banks tried to get back their loans.

The confidence of individuals was shattered. Many faced unemployment, and those in work faced reduced hours and wages. They tightened their belts and stopped spending.

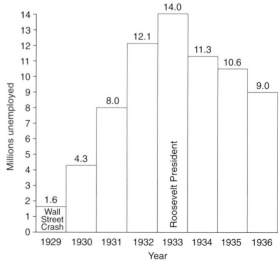

Unemployment, 1929–36.

Big institutions also suffered. About 11,000 banks stopped trading between 1929 and 1933. At the same time, demand for goods of all types fell. As a result, production fell and so did wages and jobs.

Unemployment rose dramatically, as shown in the graph on page 90.

as shown in the graph on page 90.

Revision tasks

1 In your view, what were the main causes of the Wall Street Crash? Copy and complete a summary table like the one below.

Short-term causes	Long-term causes

2 How did the Crash affect Americans? Think of four to six key words for your answer.

3 Explain the immediate effects of the Wall Street Crash.

Exam tip: q3 This is a Unit 2 question. You will need to:
- fully explain at least two consequences
- make links between each consequence
- prioritise the consequences. Which do you think was the most important and why?

Government reaction, 1929–32

President Hoover has often been criticised for his failure to deal with the immediate effects of the Great Depression.

President Hoover's actions

Hoover eventually had to take action to deal with the effects of the Depression.
- He reduced taxes, but this mainly helped the wealthy.
- He tried to help farmers with the Federal Farming Board, which purchased surplus crops in an attempt to keep up prices. This was not enough. The farmers wanted help paying their mortgages. Despite the aid, they still could not afford to pay off their loans and bankruptcies continued.
- The Federal Home Loan Bank Act, passed in July 1932, was designed to stimulate home building and increase home ownership. To do this, Hoover set up twelve regional banks with a fund of $125 million to help fund discounted home loans.

Was Hoover unfairly blamed?

Most Americans blamed President Hoover for the Crash.
- Hoover insisted that the situation was not too serious, and that 'prosperity is just around the corner'. This unfounded optimism upset many Americans.
- Hoover believed in '**rugged individualism**' and showed little sympathy for the poor, starving Americans living in shanty towns, which were nicknamed 'Hoovervilles'.
- He refused to provide federal aid for the unemployed or support a programme of public works to provide jobs for them.

Resentment among the people

With wages falling and unemployment rising, resentment grew among the American people. Hoover became very unpopular in 1932 when he ordered the US army to disperse the Bonus Marchers. These were veterans who had fought in the First World War. They had marched to Washington demanding early payment of a monetary bonus due to be paid to them in 1945. They wanted it paid early to offset the effects of the Depression. They even built a 'Hooverville' or shanty town on the edge of Washington DC. When the army tried to clear the Bonus Marchers, many were injured and two children were killed.

Revision task

List the reasons that you can find on this page to support Source 1.

SOURCE 1

Slogan of protesting farmers in Iowa.

'In Hoover we trusted, now we are busted!'

Key terms

Rugged individualism: the notion that people should overcome problems and succeed by their own efforts and hard work, not by receiving help from the government.

The impact of the Depression on people's lives

The Depression affected people both in the cities and the countryside.

The Depression in the cities

By 1933 almost one-third of the American workforce was unemployed. Once a person became unemployed it became almost impossible to secure another job. As people lost jobs they lost their homes, with some having to move into 'Hoovervilles'. Many of the unemployed simply wandered the streets or slept in doorways or cardboard boxes. Others drifted across the USA as **hobos.** It was estimated that in 1932 there were more than two million hobos.

African Americans were particularly badly affected. When the Depression began African Americans were the first to lose their jobs. Their unemployment rate had risen to 50 per cent by 1933. In addition, those who managed to keep their jobs suffered wage cuts.

The Depression also had a tremendous effect on family life.
- Young people were reluctant to take on the commitment of marriage and the number of marriages fell, as did the birth rate.
- The suicide rate rose dramatically from 12.6 per 100,000 in 1926 to 17.4 per 100,000 by 1930.
- In some states schools were closed for ten months in the year because there was not enough money to pay the teachers.

> **Key terms**
>
> **Hobos:** tramps or drifters.

The Depression in the countryside

Agriculture already faced problems in the 1920s (see page 86). However, as the Depression took hold these problems intensified.
- There were more bankruptcies as farmers were unable to sell their produce. Crops were often left to rot in the ground. Many farmers and labourers left the countryside to seek work in the towns.
- The drought of 1931 only worsened the situation. For most of the 1930s there was low rainfall and a subsequent fall in corn yields.
- The states worst hit by the drought were Texas, Oklahoma, Colorado, Kansas and New Mexico. The soil turned to dust and when the winds came there were dust storms. The affected area of 20 million hectares became known as the 'dust bowl'.
- The formation of the dust bowl forced more than 1 million people to leave their homes and seek work in the fruit-growing areas of the West coast.

> **Exam tip** Remember that the Depression affected both the cities and the countryside.

Revision tasks

1 'Hoover deserved all the criticism he got.' Make a copy of the table below and use the information in this section to complete each column.

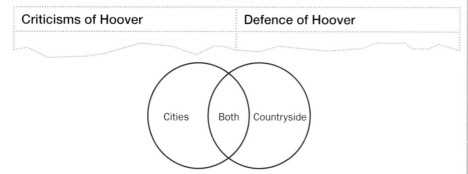

Criticisms of Hoover	Defence of Hoover

Cities · Both · Countryside

2 Make a copy of this Venn diagram. Complete the diagram by using key words to show the effects of the Depression on the cities and on the countryside. Write the effects on *both* areas in the overlapping section of the diagram.

9.4 Roosevelt and the New Deal, 1933–41

The election of Roosevelt as President brought about a change of policy known as the New Deal.

The nature of the New Deal

Roosevelt introduced a series of measures to tackle the problems of unemployment.

The election of 1932

Franklin D. Roosevelt was well educated and a talented, passionate politician. He had complete faith in his ideas for bringing the USA out of the Depression. During the presidential election campaign of 1932, his key phrase was his offer of a 'New Deal' for the American people. He won the election by a large margin: Roosevelt polled nearly 23 million votes compared to fewer than 16 million votes for Hoover. His victory was due to:

- his own promises of a New Deal
- the unpopularity of Hoover's policies in the years 1929–32.

Roosevelt's 'Hundred Days'

Due to the banking crisis and high level of unemployment, Roosevelt was determined to act quickly. From 9 March to 16 June 1933 (the 'Hundred Days') he managed to get the US **Congress** to pass a huge amount of legislation. This is summarised in the table below.

Hundred Days legislation, 9 March–16 June 1933		
Legislation	**Problem**	**Action**
Emergency Banking Act Securities Exchange Act	Americans had little confidence in the banks and might withdraw all their savings – this would lead to collapse of the banking system.	The Government declared a 'bank holiday' and closed all banks. It officially backed 5,000 banks and reassured the American people that their money was safe, restoring confidence in the banking system when the 'sound' banks were reopened eight days later. The Securities Exchange Act was set up to regulate the stock market to make sure that the speculation which caused the 1929 crash could not happen again.
Federal Emergency Relief Administration (FERA)	Poverty and unemployment	500 million dollars allocated to help relieve suffering of poor (food, clothing, etc.); seed and equipment for farmers; schemes to create jobs.
Civilian Conservation Corps (CCC)	Unemployment among young men	Men aged 18–25 given six months' work. Had to send most of their pay home to parents/wives. About 300,000 joined in 1933; by 1940, there were two million.
Public Works Administration (PWA) (became Works Progress Administration in 1935)	Unemployment	Paid for public works projects (for example, schools, roads, hospitals) and used unemployed workers.
Agricultural Adjustment Administration (AAA)	Rural poverty, unemployment and low crop prices	Advised farmers on marketing and farming techniques and helped solve problem of overproduction by government buying up produce. Farmers became more organised but wealthy farmers gained most.

Hundred Days legislation, 9 March–16 June 1933		
Legislation	Problem	Action
National Industrial Recovery Act (NIRA)	General economic condition of the USA	Set up National Recovery Administration (NRA), which set standards on working practices (hours, child labour). This helped create more jobs. Employers in the scheme displayed the eagle symbol of government approval and the Government encouraged people to use these firms. Over two million employers joined the scheme.
Tennessee Valley Authority (TVA)	Agricultural overproduction and regular flooding had ruined livelihoods of farm workers in the Tennessee Valley. No alternative jobs in industry. Area covered parts of six states and was too big for any one state to deal with.	Huge public works projects: dams, irrigation, canals and water transport. Hydroelectric power created thousands of jobs. Farmers given loans and training in soil conservation. New housing built.

The Second New Deal

As well as passing new legislation in his first hundred days of office, in later years Roosevelt updated some laws and created further legislation where it was needed.

- In 1935 the Works Progress Administration (WPA) replaced the Public Works Administration (PWA). It extended the range of employment provided, from building work to the Federal Theatre Project, which gave work to unemployed artists and writers.
- The National Labor Relations Act or Wagner Act (1935) forced employers to recognise trade unions after the National Recovery Administration was declared illegal by American courts. This law meant that workers kept the protection which the NRA had given them.
- The Social Security Act (1935) provided federal aid for the elderly and set up an unemployment insurance scheme. However, the provisions were still far less comprehensive than those in Germany or Britain.

Exam tip You will be expected to know the purpose and key features of these New Deal policies.

Revision tasks

1 Using a few key words, explain why Roosevelt won the Presidential election campaign of 1932.

2 Make a copy of the table below. Give the full title of the measures listed and use a few key words to explain what each did.

Measure	Full title	What it did
PWA		
NRA		
AAA		
CCC		
FERA		

3 Explain how Roosevelt's New Deal policies changed the plight of the unemployed in the years 1933–41.

Exam tip: q3 This is a Unit 2 question. You will need to:
- fully explain at least two changes
- make links between each change
- prioritise the changes. Which do you think was the most important and why?

Opposition to the New Deal

There were a number of groups in the USA who were critical of the New Deal.

Business leaders

They were unhappy about various aspects of the New Deal:
- regulations on working conditions
- the growth of trade unions and their increasing power
- the huge cost of the welfare programmes (which came from taxes paid by Americans).

The states

Some states were concerned about the New Deal because:
- measures like the TVA cut right across the rights of individual states
- they feared that the Federal Government was becoming too powerful.

Politicians

Some politicians opposed the New Deal.
- Republicans (not surprisingly) bitterly opposed the Democrat Roosevelt.
- Even some conservative Democrats opposed him.
- Some radicals in the USA, like Huey Long, believed the New Deal did not go far enough.

The Supreme Court

The Supreme Court clashed with Roosevelt.
- Its judges (mainly old and Republican) ruled that several of the New Deal measures were illegal.
- Matters came to a head in 1937 when Roosevelt wanted to appoint six new judges to alter the political balance of the Court in favour of the Democrats. This plan failed but afterwards Supreme Court opposition lessened.

> ### Revision task
> Make a copy of this pie chart. Prioritise the four different groups who opposed the New Deal by placing the most important in the largest section down to the least important in the smallest. Use key words in each section to explain your decisions.

The extent of recovery

The New Deal did bring some improvements but was not a total success.

Exam tip Ensure you give a balanced judgement on the achievements of the New Deal. It was neither a total success nor a total failure.

Assessing the New Deal

Weaknesses	Successes
• When Roosevelt cut back his programmes in 1937 unemployment rose dramatically. • He never fully conquered unemployment in the 1930s; unemployment was only solved by the USA's entry into the Second World War in 1941. • The USA's trade (and the world's trade) did not recover. • Roosevelt failed to convince even his own supporters of the need to change the organisation of the Supreme Court to stop it opposing his reforms. • African Americans gained relatively little from the New Deal.	• In the USA the Depression did not lead to extreme movements such as Communism or fascism taking hold. Roosevelt restored the American people's faith in democracy. • Many millions of jobs were created and vital relief (food, shelter, clothing) was supplied to the poor. • Agriculture and industry benefited from efficient infrastructure (roads, services).

Revision tasks

1 Make a copy of this set of scales (right). On the scales, summarise the successes and weaknesses of the New Deal.

2 Overall, do you think the New Deal was successful in solving the social and economic problems of the USA 1933–41? Use a few key words to record your opinion.

Successes   Weaknesses

3

SOURCE 2

From a history of the USA published in 2009.

The American economy greatly benefited from the First World War. In the 1920s America enjoyed an economic boom which was encouraged by the policies of the Republican presidents as well as the advanced techniques that the car industry began to use. There was a rapid growth in new industries and a dramatic rise in the values of shares on the US stock market.

What can you learn from Source 2 about the reasons for the economic boom of the 1920s?

Exam tip: q3 This is a Unit 2 inference question. That means you have to find at least one inference or message and back it up with evidence from the source. Begin your answer with 'This source suggests …'.

Key content

You need to have a good working knowledge of the following areas:

- the causes and consequences of the economic boom
- mass production and the Ford Motor Company
- hire purchase and the stock market boom
- declining industries and the problems of agriculture
- Hollywood, jazz and changes in entertainment
- changes in the position of women, especially the flappers
- prohibition and the gangsters
- the Jim Crow laws and the Ku Klux Klan
- Sacco and Vanzetti and the Monkey Trial
- the long- and short-term causes of the Wall Street Crash
- the immediate effects of the Crash
- Hoover's attempts to deal with the Depression
- the effects of the Depression on cities and the countryside
- the key features of Roosevelt's First and Second New Deal
- opposition to the New Deal
- the successes and weaknesses of the New Deal.

During this period Britain experienced major social reforms under the Liberal governments, became involved in the First World War and experienced the only ever British general strike.

Key issues

As with all examination topics, you will be expected to do more than simply learn the content and write it out again. You will need to show understanding of key issues from the period. These are:

- votes for women and social reform
- the part played by Britain on the Western Front
- the Home Front and social change
- economic and social change, 1918–29.

10.1 Votes for women and social reform

In the years before 1914 the Liberals brought in a series of social welfare measures whilst women campaigned for the right to vote.

Votes for women

At the beginning of the twentieth century, women in Britain played little part in political life. They were not able to vote in general elections or stand for Parliament. Three different societies campaigned for the vote for women in the years before 1914.

The National Union of Women's Suffrage Societies (NUWSS)

The National Union of Women's Suffrage Societies was set up in 1897 by Millicent Fawcett and had 500 or more branches throughout the country. Fawcett was a suffragist. Suffragists believed that women would get the vote eventually. The NUWSS issued pamphlets, presented petitions and organised marches and meetings. Fawcett thought it was crucial to keep the issue of women's suffrage in the public eye.

The Women's Freedom League (WFL)

The Women's Freedom League was set up in 1907 by Charlotte Despard. Members were not as peaceful as the suffragists and were prepared to break the law as long as it did not lead to violence. Their methods included the following:

- In 1911 members refused to take part in the census, the official population count. They broke the law by refusing to fill in the census form.
- Others chained themselves to the railings outside the House of Commons.
- Members refused to pay taxes, arguing that they were not represented in Parliament. For this, their property was sold to pay what was owing.
- Muriel Matters, a member of the WFL, hired an airship and flew over the Houses of Parliament, throwing out carrots and propaganda leaflets.

> ### Comment
>
> *On 9 February 1907 about 4,000 women walked from Hyde Park to the Exeter Hall in the Strand. Unfortunately it poured with rain all day and the long skirts and dresses of the women were soon covered with mud. This was why it was nicknamed the 'mud march'. The women who took part showed great bravery in the face of some hostile male onlookers.*

The Women's Social and Political Union (WSPU)

In 1903 Mrs Emmeline Pankhurst founded a new organisation, the Women's Social and Political Union, which was determined to use more extreme, even militant, methods to get publicity and secure the vote more quickly. The *Daily Mail* nicknamed these more extreme campaigners 'suffragettes' and the name stuck. They used a variety of methods:

- WSPU militancy began in 1905 when they interrupted meetings of Liberals and were arrested.
- On 5 July 1909, the imprisoned suffragette Marion Wallace Dunlop went on hunger strike.
- In March 1912 the WSPU began a stone-throwing campaign in the centre of London to gain even more publicity for the cause of votes for women.
- On 5 June 1913, Emily Wilding Davison, in order to get maximum publicity, decided to rush out and pin a suffragette banner on the King's horse, Anmer, while he was competing in the Derby at Epsom race course. As the horses rounded Tattenham Corner, Davison rushed in front of Anmer, only to be hit by the horse and killed.
- In the years 1912–14 the suffragettes escalated their violence. They cut telephone wires, set fire to derelict buildings and post boxes, poured purple dye into reservoirs, poured acid on the greens of golf courses and slashed paintings in art galleries. They frequently attacked and assaulted leading Liberals, especially Prime Minister Asquith.

> **Exam tip** The WSPU is generally well known. Do not forgot the methods and activities of the other two societies.

How did the authorities react?

The Liberals had to deal with the problems of hunger-striking and increasing suffragette militancy.

- The prison authorities were afraid that a suffragette might die in prison. This would give the suffragette movement even more publicity, so they began force-feeding the prisoners.
- More and more suffragettes were arrested, went on hunger strike and were force-fed. In 1913 the Government introduced the Temporary Discharge Bill which was nicknamed the 'Cat and Mouse Act'. Prisoners on hunger strike were released when very ill and sent back to prison when they had recovered.

> **Comment**
>
> *In many respects the activities of the suffragettes, designed to gain the vote for women, had the opposite effect. Their extreme militant activities convinced many people that women were not responsible enough to have the vote. The suffragettes also made it difficult for Asquith, the Prime Minister, to introduce any such measure without looking as if he was giving in to violence.*

> ### Revision task
>
> Make a copy of the following table and use the information from this section to complete it. Give each society a rating out of 5 (with 5 being very effective) for the methods used. Briefly explain each decision.
>
> | Society | Leader | Methods | Rating (1–5) |
> |---------|--------|---------|--------------|
> | NUWSS | | | |
> | WFL | | | |
> | WSPU | | | |

Child welfare measures and OAPs

The Liberals introduced a series of measures to help the young and the old.

Child welfare measures

The Liberals believed it was very important for the children of the poor to be looked after properly. If parents could not do this, then it was the responsibility of the state. They brought in a series of reforms, including:

- *1906 School Meals Act.* This instructed local authorities to pay for school meals for the poorest children – for those pupils 'unable, by lack of food, to take advantage of the education provided for them'. By 1914, over 150,000 children a year were receiving free school meals.
- *1907 School Medical Service.* Most children of the poor never saw a doctor. The Government ruled that every local authority had to provide a school medical service. The Government paid for school clinics, where treatment was free. Regular health inspections in schools helped doctors treat skin and hair diseases, such as scabies and impetigo.
- *1908 Children's Charter.* This prevented children under the age of sixteen from buying cigarettes and entering pubs. Parents could be taken to court if they were cruel to their children or allowed them to go begging.

Old age pensions

In 1908, old age pensions were included in the first budget of Lloyd George, the new Chancellor of the Exchequer. The first pensions were claimed on 1 January 1909.

- Pensions were paid to all old people over the age of 70 who had an income of less than twelve shillings (60p) a week. This was over 60 per cent of all people over 70.
- Pensions were paid on a sliding scale of between one shilling (5p) and five shillings (25p) a week depending on the old person's income.
- The money for these pensions came from government funds.

However, there were some criticisms of the new pensions. Some argued that the age restriction seemed too high. Not many people lived until the age of 70 and five shillings was not enough to live on.

> **Comment**
>
> *Over 650,000 people applied for a pension in the first year and by the start of the First World War in 1914 there were almost one million pensioners. With the pension the fear of the workhouse almost disappeared. By 1912, the number of people over 70 years old in the workhouses had dropped by 5,590.*

Labour exchanges and the National Insurance Act

The Liberals also wanted to help the unemployed and those workers who were not insured against sickness.

Labour exchanges

To help the unemployed find work, the President of the Board of Trade, Winston Churchill, pushed through the Labour Exchanges Act of 1909. The idea was to save unemployed people having to tramp from one factory to another in search of work. Labour exchanges, nowadays known as job centres, would advertise job vacancies. By 1913, there were 430 labour exchanges throughout Britain.

Unemployment and health insurance

In 1911, the Liberals introduced the National Insurance Act which provided insurance against unemployment and sickness.

Unemployment insurance

At first this insurance applied to under three million people in trades where workers were often laid off, such as the building industry.

- Workers, employers and the state each paid the equivalent of 1p each week into an insurance fund.
- In return, workers could claim seven shillings (35p) a week for up to fifteen weeks, provided they could work and had paid sufficient contributions into the fund. The scheme was extended to another eight million people in 1920.

Health insurance

This was an insurance scheme against ill-health.

- It applied to all male workers who earned less than £3 a week – this was the majority of the working classes.

> **Comment**
>
> *Initial criticisms of unemployment insurance were that it applied only to 3 million workers, and members of the Labour Party disliked the fact that poorly paid workers had to make a weekly contribution.*

- Workers paid 4d (nearly 2p) a week into the scheme, the employer 3d and the state 2d. This led to the slogan, '9 pence for 4 pence'.
- In return, a worker could claim 'free' medical treatment and ten shillings a week for a maximum of 26 weeks if unable to work. After that a disability pension of five shillings could be awarded.
- A male worker's wife was given a special payment of 30 shillings (£1.50) after the birth of a baby.

The scheme proved of real benefit to the poorest workers who could not afford to visit a doctor. However, it brought bitter opposition from doctors who insisted that they would not be paid fairly for their work. The scheme did not apply to the self-employed, wives, domestic servants or women workers (it was extended to women workers in 1920). Again, some critics said that ten shillings a week was insufficient.

Revision tasks

1 Make a copy of the table below. Use the information in this section to explain the main terms and importance of the following reforms.

	Terms	Importance
Child welfare		
Old age pensions		
Labour exchanges		
Unemployment insurance		
Health insurance		

2 What can you learn from Source 1 about the activities of the suffragettes?

> ## SOURCE 1
> The Speaker of the House of Commons, writing in 1925.
> *The activities of the militant suffragettes had now [1913] reached the stage at which nothing was safe from their attacks. Churches were burnt, public buildings and private residences were destroyed, bombs were exploded, the police and individuals were assaulted, meetings broken up, and every imaginable device resorted to. The feeling in the House of Commons, caused by the lawless actions of the militants, hardened the opposition to their demands.*

Exam tip: q2 This is a Unit 3 inference question. An inference means what the source is suggesting, what messages it is giving.
- You need to make at least two inferences.
- Support each inference with evidence from the source.

10.2 The part played by Britain on the Western Front

The war began in August 1914 when Germany attacked France via Belgium, using the long-prepared **Schlieffen Plan**. On Tuesday 4 August 1914, Britain declared war on Germany. The armies of the Great Powers in Europe were already on the march. Britain was honouring its agreement in a treaty of 1839 to protect Belgium if the country was invaded.

The British Expeditionary Force (BEF), 1914

The BEF of 100,000 men was well-equipped and left Britain within a week – quicker than the Germans had expected. The German advance had already been held up in Belgium, and the BEF had no difficulty in landing at ports on the French-Belgian border. Even so, the Germans advanced into France, towards the River Marne, and the capital, Paris, was very close.

Key terms

Schlieffen Plan: the plan devised by the German commander Schlieffen in 1904 to fight a war on two fronts.

The French responded quickly by moving many of their troops to stop the German attack. Paris taxis were used to move troops quickly to prevent German troops reaching the capital. The result was battles in the autumn of 1914, such as the Battle of the Marne, which lasted for a week in September. The BEF fought bravely alongside the French in these battles, but suffered heavy losses. By December 1914, over half of the original BEF were dead.

The Germans made a last desperate attempt at a quick victory in the west by advancing towards the Channel ports of Calais and Boulogne. However, the British forces, having moved from the Marne area, met them near the town of Ypres. After six weeks of furious fighting, the town remained in Allied hands and the ports were safe. Both sides suffered huge casualties, and both had to prepare themselves for a longer war than had been anticipated.

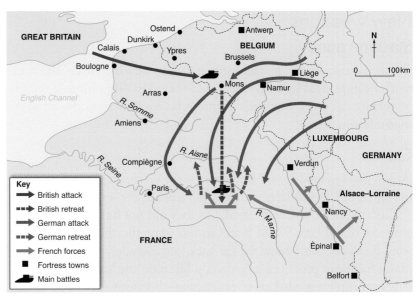

The Battle of the Marne, September 1914.

> **Exam tip** Remember you need to know the part played by the BEF in defeating the Schlieffen Plan and the German advance in 1914.

Britain and the Western Front, 1915–17

There was trench warfare on the Western Front between 1915 and 1917, with neither side able to break through.

Trench warfare

Both sides began to 'dig in' in order to defend themselves from the enemy. By Christmas 1914, it was clear that neither side was going to achieve a quick victory. The war had become one of stalemate. During the winter of 1914–15, two million soldiers faced each other across No Man's Land. Their rows of trenches became more organised and sophisticated as the months went by, as both armies sought some protection against both the weather and enemy machine-gun fire. No Man's Land was fortified with barbed wire and machine-gun posts. Before long, it was a wilderness of muddy shell craters, often containing rotting corpses.

The continuous line of trenches from the North Sea ports to the Swiss border made it impossible to outflank the enemy. A decisive victory could only by gained by a successful direct assault, and then breaking through into open country behind enemy lines. For three years, generals on both sides believed that this was possible if sufficient numbers of troops were assembled, and if there was enough bombardment of the area to be attacked. This was tried in 1915, but with heavy casualties. At the Battle of Loos in September 1915, the British suffered 80,000 fatalities in less than two weeks. The line of trenches hardly moved at all.

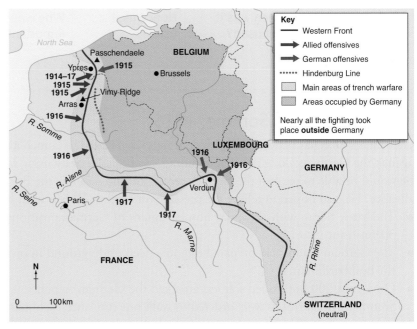

Trench warfare on the Western Front.

New weapons

Machine guns

On the battlefield, the machine gun had a devastating effect. The water-cooled machine guns used by both sides could fire up to 600 rounds a minute and frequently cut down hundreds of troops before they were able to advance more than a few metres.

Gas

Poison gas was used for the first time by the Germans at the Second Battle of Ypres in April 1915. It was later used by both sides in the war.

Gas attacks were widely feared, but they did not have a major impact on the outcome of the First World War. Gas was unpredictable in battle – a change in wind direction could blow the gas back to the sender – and by 1917 effective gas masks had been produced to protect soldiers on the battlefield.

Most people regarded gas as a particularly horrific weapon. In fact, the use of poison gas in war had been banned by international agreements at The Hague in 1899 and 1907.

> ### Comment
> *There were different kinds of gas: chlorine and phosgene gas destroyed the victim's lungs, mustard gas was particularly horrible and destroyed flesh.*

Tanks

The British used tanks for the first time at the Battle of the Somme in September 1916. The tanks achieved a little success at first but there were not enough of them to break the stalemate on the Western Front.

The first tanks were armour-plated with cannon and machine guns and moved at 5 km per hour. These models were unreliable and often broke down. Those that were successful often advanced too quickly for supporting troops and were captured or destroyed. At the Battle of Cambrai in 1917 the British used 381 tanks with great success in the initial stages of the battle. But the infantry soldiers could not keep up with them and in the later stages of the battle much of the land captured by the tank crews was recaptured by the Germans. Only in the final few months of the war in 1918 did tanks play an important part in bringing the stalemate on the Western Front to an end.

> **Exam tip** Do not just revise details of these new weapons. You must be able to explain their effectiveness on the Western Front.

> ### Revision task
> Make a copy of the table below. Use the information in this section to complete it.
>
> | Type of weapon | When was it first used? | How was it used? | Why was it important? |
> |---|---|---|---|
> | | | | |

The Battle of the Somme, 1916

General Sir Douglas Haig, the British commander, decided to launch a major attack against the Germans along the River Somme. He hoped that by using heavy artillery he would be able to weaken the German front line and so allow the British troops to advance. He also hoped to relieve the pressure on Verdun. This is what happened.

- The battle began with a five-day bombardment of German positions along a 30 km front.
- The German troops had prepared dugouts deep underground in order to survive the bombardment.
- On 1 July, 200,000 Allied soldiers attacked the German trenches along the Somme. British troops were ordered to walk not run since each man was carrying up to 30 kg of equipment.

- In the ten minutes between the end of the bombardment and the British attack, the Germans were able to return to their trenches and machine guns.
- On the first day of the battle, the British lost 20,000 men with another 40,000 wounded.

The Battle of the Somme ended in the middle of November 1916. Only 14 km of land had been gained by the Allies, at a cost of 600,000 casualties. At the end of 1916, there was still no breakthrough on the Western Front.

The wisdom of British tactics has been debated ever since. Sir Douglas Haig, the British general in charge of the offensive, has been ridiculed by many writers, but his reputation has been defended by others.

The end of the war

The Western Front, 1918: victory for the Allies

In April 1917, the USA joined the Allies in the war against Germany. The Germans knew it would take time for the USA to recruit and train an army, so they drew up plans to win a swift victory before the full impact of the American army was felt on the Western Front.

By March 1918, the Russian army had been defeated on the Eastern Front. The Germans could now move a million of their own men to the Western Front.

- Ludendorff, the German commander, decided that since he now had many more men than the Allies, he must make an all-out attack on the Western Front before large numbers of American troops arrived in Europe.
- On 21 March 1918, the Ludendorff offensive began and the Germans advanced rapidly; they had soon moved forward 65 km along a 130 km front.
- They reached the River Marne in July and once again the French capital looked as if it might fall to the Germans.

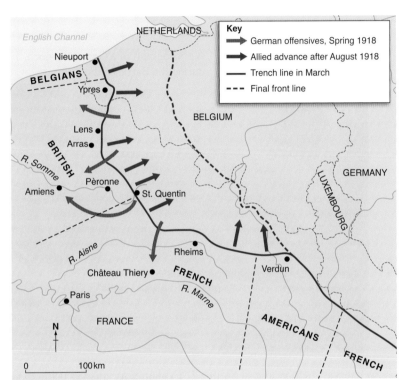

Europe in the final stages of the war.

The Allied commander at the time, General Foch, began his counter-attack on 18 July and with the help of newly arrived American troops was able to reverse the German advance.

- In August, the British defeated the Germans at Amiens with the help of tanks.
- More victories followed in Flanders (for example, at Ypres).

On 4 October, with the German army in full retreat, Ludendorff asked the Allies for a truce. On 11 November an armistice was signed and the First World War was over.

Revision tasks

1 Make a copy of the following table. In column 2 use key words to summarise the part played by the British. In column 3 judge how important each event was for the outcome of the war on a scale of 1 to 5, with 5 being the most important. Give a brief explanation for each decision.

Event	Part played by British	Importance (1–5)
The BEF and 1914		
The Somme, 1916		
The events of 1918		

2

SOURCE 2

A photograph of a German trench, 1 July 1916, during the Battle of the Somme.

What was the purpose of Source 2? Explain your answer using details from the source and your own knowledge.

Exam tip: q2 You need to explain:
- What is the source suggesting?
- What message is it trying to get across?
- What was its purpose? What is it trying to make people think or do?

10.3 The Home Front and social change

The First World War brought important changes on the Home Front.

DORA, censorship and propaganda

The powers of the Government increased during the First World War.

DORA

During the First World War, the Government imposed regulations and censorship that limited what people could do or say. The Defence of the Realm Act (DORA) was passed in August 1914. Its list of restrictions grew as the war went on.

DORA's measures were intended to provide for the efficient government of the country and to make sure that no help was given to the enemy. Measures included allowing the Government to take over any factory or workshop, to censor newspapers, to limit the hours pubs could open and even to water down beer.

Exam tip You do not have to revise all of these measures. Make sure you know three or four.

Censorship and propaganda

To improve morale, newspapers were encouraged to print stories of British and Allied heroism and bravery, giving the impression that the war was being fought with huge successes. No pictures of dead soldiers were allowed to be printed.

However, the long lists of official deaths and of missing soldiers increasingly showed how biased the reporting was.

Propaganda continued to be produced throughout the war – pamphlets, posters, newspaper reports and adverts. These gave the impression that the Germans were evil, and the British should be proud to participate in the German defeat. From the autumn of 1914, storied circulated about German atrocities in Belgium – women had been shot for no reason; babies had been bayoneted; nuns had been raped. Newspapers in France, Britain and the USA circulated the stories, and Belgian refugees added their own accounts. Whilst some civilians did suffer, the extent of the suffering was greatly exaggerated for propaganda purposes. The Germans were nicknamed 'Huns' – the name of a barbaric people who lived during the fourth to the fifth centuries AD. Many people wanted to believe that Germans of the early twentieth century were similarly cruel and evil.

Only later in the war did the Government begin to allow a more realistic picture to be presented. For example, it released an official film of the Battle of the Somme to be shown at cinemas. Some people fainted during its screening, even though it did not come anywhere near to showing the full extent of the horror.

Recruitment and rationing

The Government also had to deal with the problems of recruitment for the armed forces and food shortages.

Recruitment

The War Minister, Lord Kitchener, planned to rely on volunteers to enlarge the army. There were 175,000 volunteer recruits by the end of September 1914, and from then on an average of 125,000 a month. There were many reasons why so many men were keen to join up. Some were motivated by patriotism, others because war seemed to promise adventure in an age when there were few opportunities to travel. Many were simply escaping from poverty and unemployment.

Men reluctant to join the armed forces were shamed into doing so. In London, some women handed out white feathers to any young man not in uniform. Public speakers whipped up enthusiasm in the crowd, with men encouraged to sign up there and then while influenced by the excitement of the moment.

However, as the war went on, there was a shortage of recruits. This was partly because there were not so many men eligible to volunteer, but it was also because the real horrors of war were becoming better understood. So in January 1916, the Government passed an act allowing all single men between the ages of 18 and 41 to be called up for active service. This was extended to all married men of the same age group later in the year.

Conscientious objectors

Some men, known as conscientious objectors, refused to join up because they thought it was wrong to fight and kill. The media and a good part of the public had little sympathy for such men – they were seen as cowards. Some conscientious objectors were prepared to work in the war effort in a non-fighting role (for example, as ambulance men) but others refused to have anything to do with the war, and were imprisoned on the assumption that they could be spies.

Rationing

At the beginning of the war there was a shortage of food as many people rushed to stockpile supplies. After this initial panic, supplied settled down for a while, helped by the measures taken by the Government under DORA. However, Britain relied on imports for much of its food, and German submarine operations effectively blocked much of this supply. The situation became acute in 1917 when German

Comment

A significant proportion of men fought in 'Pals Battalions' where groups of friends were deliberately kept together. Whilst this was good for morale in the trenches, the effect back home was horrific when a whole regiment was killed in an attack.

Comment

Other men were encouraged to stay at home – for example, coal miners and train drivers – as they were essential for maintaining basic services on the Home Front.

submarines successfully attacked supply ships crossing the Atlantic. In response, the Government tried to operate a voluntary rationing scheme, with limits on bread, meat and sugar. However, this was unsuccessful and the shortages continued.

Desperate attempts were made to grow more food. Grassed areas were turned into vegetable patches, as were public parks. In fact, over two and a half million acres of land were ploughed up for growing vegetables or keeping animals. Much of the work in the fields was undertaken by the new Women's Land Army because a large proportion of farm workers had volunteered to fight at the front.

In spite of all the Government's attempts to solve the food shortages, a limited form of rationing was introduced in 1918. Meat, sugar, butter, cheese and margarine had to be obtained with a ration card at the butcher's and grocer's shop with which a person was registered. Each person was allowed fifteen ounces (425 g) of meat per week, five ounces (140 g) of bacon and four ounces (110 g) of butter or margarine. This rationing system worked and food queues disappeared. It is also claimed that at the end of the war poorer people were healthier than they had been at the beginning of the war, partly as a result of getting a fairer share of healthy food through rationing.

Revision task

Draw a mind map to summarise government policies during the First World War, including DORA, censorship, propaganda, recruitment and rationing.

The part played by women

Women played an important part in the war effort.

Women before the war

Before the war started, British women mostly accepted the role given to them – that is, to look after the home and bring up children.

Women and the war

In 1914, the war started to have a major impact on the position of women in British society, and on their attitude towards themselves. During the war about five million men joined the army. With so many men away fighting (and nearly one million not returning alive), there was a huge shortage of workers, especially in the jobs traditionally done by men. Women worked in the following areas:

- War work: in factories and steel mills; driving buses; building ships; or working in agriculture in the Women's Land Army.
- New war work: large numbers of women worked in munitions factories, making bullets and shells for ammunition. The number increased from 200,000 in 1914 to nearly one million in 1918. The work was highly dangerous; sometimes there were major explosions. The chemicals that women worked with tended to turn their skin yellow, and they were nicknamed 'canaries'. Industrial work was well paid compared with before 1914 (even allowing for rises in prices for scarce goods). In munitions factories women could earn about £4 per week, compared with £2 a month as a domestic servant.
- The armed services: women were allowed to join up from April 1917 onwards. About 100,000 joined the following organisations:
  - Women's Army Auxiliary Corps (WAAC)
  - Women's Royal Naval Service (WRNS or Wrens)
  - Women's Royal Air Force (WRAF).
  Most of the woman who entered the armed forces took over clerical and administrative duties normally done by men, releasing men to fight at the front.
- Nurses: about 23,000 women volunteered to serve as nurses close to the front line, often working in France or Belgium.
- Volunteer Aid Detachment: this provided cooks, kitchen maids, laundry workers and drivers.

The work done by many women affected their status. Many were receiving their own wage packet for the first time, making them financially independent. Some adapted their social behaviour and changed their style of dress, even daring to wear trousers. Others were more willing to go out on their own, even going into pubs, drinking alcohol and smoking in public.

During the war, the suffragettes suspended their campaign of violence and fully co-operated with the war effort. Increasingly, women were seen by men as sensible, and more capable of making decisions.

Women at the end of the war

The loyalty and service of women during the war was recognised by the all-male British Government. In 1918, the Representation of the People Act gave the vote to women over the age of 30. (Men could vote at the age of 21.) In 1919, women were allowed to do jury service, become lawyers and join the Civil Service. (Only in 1928 did women get the vote on the same terms as men.)

On the other hand, when the war ended, women were forced to give up many of the jobs they had taken over. It was thought to be only fair that returning soldiers were treated as heroes and given priority.

> **Exam tip** Remember to give a balanced answer if asked about the effects of the First World War on the position of women. They gained the vote and the confidence of doing 'men's jobs' but generally went back to their pre-war jobs and roles afterwards.

Revision tasks

1 Make a copy of the following table. Complete it with key words to show the changes to the position of women as a result of the First World War.

Women before the war	Women during the war	Women after the war

2

SOURCE 3

A government poster issued in 1917.

How useful is Source 3 as evidence of the methods used by the Government to deal with food shortages?

> **Exam tip: q2** You need to evaluate:
> - what is useful about the source and what it suggests about the Government's methods
> - what its limitations are in what it shows and suggests, bringing in your own contextual knowledge of government methods
> - what is useful and what the limitations are of the purpose of the poster – or why it was used.

10.4 Economic and social change, 1918–29

During the 1920s there were further changes in the role of women, whilst the Government had to deal with serious industrial unrest culminating in the General Strike of 1926.

The changing role of women, 1918–28

During the 1920s women did make some progress, especially in their political and social position. However, there was little or no change in employment opportunities.

Political progress

- There was some progress in the political position, with women aged 30 and over getting the vote in 1918. However, younger women, in their twenties, were disappointed with the age limit. They were considered too young and immature to cope in a responsible way with the vote. The real reason was that men feared a female majority of voters.
- Women also won the right to stand for Parliament and in 1919 Nancy Astor became the first woman MP to take her seat in Parliament. In 1928 women aged 21 and over were given the vote. At last they had equal voting rights to men.
- In 1929 Margaret Bondfield became the first female member of government.

Social progress

The war had given many women greater confidence and changed their attitude to their appearance and social habits.

- Young women no longer had chaperones. They were able to go to the cinema or to dances with boyfriends without having to take an aunt or other female with them.
- The flapper was the most extreme example of these social changes. These were young women, in their twenties, who challenged the old-fashioned ideas about women. They wore revealing clothes with short skirts, a lot of make-up and short hair. They drank and smoked in public and performed modern dances such as the Charleston.

Employment opportunities

After the First World War women returned to their traditional, unskilled, low paid jobs or their roles as housewives. By the 1930s women's wages were only half those of men, even if they were doing the same job.

However, there was some progress:

- The Sex Disqualification Removal Act of 1919 meant that women could no longer be barred from any job because of their sex. In theory, they could now enter professions such as law and architecture. However, the law still only applied to single women. Once married, a woman had to give up her job.
- In 1925 the Civil Service admitted women to government service for the first time.

> **Exam tip** Answers on the progress of women are often generalised and vague. Remember to revise key developments such as the Sex Disqualification Removal Act. This will impress an examiner.

Revision tasks

1 Make a copy of the set of scales shown here. Use key words to make notes on each pan indicating progress, and lack of progress, for women.

2 Overall do you think women made progress in the 1920s? Explain your answer.

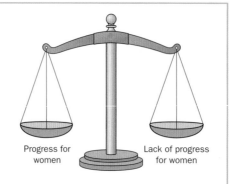

Progress for women   Lack of progress for women

Industrial unrest, 1918–26

In 1926, there was a general strike which lasted for nine days. This was due to problems in the coal industry and developments in the trade union movement.

Problems in the coal industry

During the First World War, the Government nationalised, or took over, the coal mines. This benefited the miners because they got:

- a seven-hour day
- a national minimum wage (the same wages for every miner, no matter which pit he worked in).

Coal mining, however, suffered in the years after the First World War.

- Exports of British coal, which before the war had been 100 million tons a year, fell as British coal had to compete with the cheaper coal produced by countries such as the USA, Germany and Poland.
- The miners wanted the Government to permanently nationalise the coal industry. In 1919, the Prime Minister, Lloyd George, set up the Sankey Commission to look into the coal industry and promised to accept its findings. In 1920, it recommended permanent nationalisation. Lloyd George went back on his word and would not accept this conclusion.
- When the coal industry faced a serious slump in the winter of 1920–21 and began to lose five million pounds a month, the Government handed the industry back to private owners. Their solution was to cut the miners' pay and make them work a longer day.

The trade union movement

The trade union movement grew larger and stronger in the years before and after the First World War.

Some trade unions at this time believed that strike action was the most effective way of bringing about changes in society. Their ultimate weapon was 'direct action', or strikes culminating in a national or general strike. The British trade unions moved closer to this idea with the formation of the Triple Industrial Alliance in 1913.

- The three largest unions, the Miners' Federation of Great Britain (MFGB), the Transport Workers' Federation (mainly dockworkers) and the National Union of Railwaymen, agreed that if one member came out on strike the other two would come out in sympathy.
- This would effectively lead to a general strike as the country would be paralysed.

The Triple Alliance was abandoned during the First World War but trade unions increased their strength as membership doubled from four to eight million between 1914 and 1920. There was a great number of strikes in the period 1919–20 and the Triple Alliance was revived in February 1919.

Exam tip Remember that the General Strike was not just caused by problems in the coal industry. Industrial militancy and the Triple Alliance also played their part.

Black Friday, 15 April 1921

There was almost a general strike in 1921.

- In April 1921, the coal industry owners announced wage cuts and a longer working day. They locked out the miners until they agreed to these terms. The longer working day did not make sense. It meant that miners would produce even more coal that could not be sold.
- The MFGB called upon the transport workers and the railwaymen to support them in a strike against the wage cut on Friday 15 April.
- At the very last moment, however, these two unions pulled out, leaving the miners to fight on alone. That is why the miners called it 'Black Friday'.
- The Triple Alliance, which was now known at the 'Cripple Alliance', collapsed. The miners were eventually starved back to work in July 1921. They had to accept pay cuts and the addition of an extra 30 minutes to the working day.

Red Friday, 31 July 1925

Coal prices continued to fall, leading to the second occasion when there could have been a general strike.

- The pit owners again announced a longer working day and pay cuts. The miners' leader, A. J. Cook, was furious. His reply, 'Not a penny off the pay! Not a minute on the day!' became the miners' slogan.
- The Trades Union Congress (TUC) backed the miners. All movement of coal by land or water was to be stopped from 31 July.
- The Conservative Prime Minister, Stanley Baldwin, was not ready for a general strike. He therefore gave a subsidy, or financial support, to the coal owners to last nine months and to prevent a cut in wages. In the meantime, he set up another commission, led by the Liberal Herbert Samuel, to study the problems in the coal industry and come up with a long-term solution.
- The unions called their success 'Red Friday'. It was, however, only a breathing space. Everyone knew there would be a showdown if the miners and pit owners did not agree about what was to happen when the Government subsidy ended on 1 May 1926.
- Meanwhile, the Government made preparations for a general strike.

The immediate cause of the strike

The Samuel Commission reported in March 1926 but failed to find a solution that would keep either side happy.

Shortly after the commission reported, Baldwin announced that the subsidy would end on 30 April. The owners then set wages even lower than they had previously proposed. The miners refused to accept this and were again locked out. They called on the other unions to support them by coming out on strike. The TUC agreed to support the miners and to negotiate with the Government on their behalf.

On 30 April 1926, the employers made their final offer –a thirteen per cent wage cut and a 'temporary' increase in the working day by one hour. It was rejected by the MFGB. On the following day, the TUC voted by a large majority in favour of striking in support of the miners. Talks between the TUC and Baldwin continued in an effort to find a solution. These were called off by Baldwin on 2 May when he heard that the printers at the offices of the *Daily Mail* had refused to print an article, 'For King and Country', which criticised the miners. The strike began at midnight on 3 May.

Exam tip The miners were locked out in April 1926. The other unions then came out on strike in sympathy with the miners.

The General Strike of 1926

This lasted for nine days and brought much of the country to a standstill.

At first, the strike seemed successful and in the first few days the number of strikers actually increased. The strikers were well organised. They allowed essential supplies and had no intention of bringing out hospital workers or other key workers. There was little trouble and only one person was killed in the first week. However, scenes of violence gradually increased. In Glasgow and Doncaster strikers were arrested, tried and imprisoned. There were police baton charges, stone throwing, attempted derailment of trains driven by volunteers and overturned lorries and buses.

Much to the surprise of the miners and most strikers, the TUC did not extend the strike. Instead, on 12 May its leaders went to Downing Street and called off the strike.

The work of volunteers

Many middle-class people disagreed with the idea of a general strike and volunteered to help the Government. For some people, jobs such as driving buses were 'good fun'. Such people managed to keep some buses and trains running.

Government preparations

The Government had been preparing for a general strike since Red Friday, July 1925, and by May 1926 it had a list of 100,000 volunteers prepared to help with essential services during a strike. During the strike the Government used the army to escort food convoys and guard the food depot set up in Hyde Park. Special constables were recruited to help keep law and order.

Government propaganda

The Government printed its own newspaper during the strike, the *British Gazette*. The chairman of the BBC, Sir John Reith, decided to allow only broadcasts by the Government and he refused airtime to the TUC and the Labour Party leader, Ramsey MacDonald. The Government even placed loudspeakers in streets to ensure more people heard the Government version of events. The strike was portrayed as a threat to the British system of government – an attempt by a minority of the people to bully the majority. The Government insisted that the strike was not working and it praised the work of the volunteers.

The attitude of the general public

Public support was very important – it would decide the outcome of the strike. Government propaganda successfully convinced many that the strike was a threat to government and was wrong.

Why the strike failed

Stanley Baldwin

The Prime Minister played an important role. He broadcast every day on the radio and spoke in a very matter-of-fact, common-sense way. He did not attack the miners and insisted he wanted to help them, but argued that a general strike was not the way. Above all else, he refused to talk to the TUC until they called off the strike.

TUC mistakes

The TUC did not get their message across to most of the public because they were not allowed to broadcast on the BBC. Their own newspaper, the *British Worker*, was not well distributed and did not reach the north-east until 12 May, the last day of the strike. The TUC was looking for a way out. On 10 May, it asked the miners' leaders to accept the Samuel Commission's recommendations. When the miners refused, the TUC met the Prime Minister and called off the strike.

The results of the General Strike

- The miners were left to fight on alone. Some began to drift back to work in August 1926 and the majority had returned by December. They had to accept the pay cut and the longer working day. The problems of the coal industry had not been solved. Indeed, they were now even worse due to the exports lost during the strike.
- Calling off the General Strike lowered confidence in the TUC. Many workers were penalised when they returned to work. Ringleaders were sacked and others had to accept inferior terms of employment. Baldwin passed the Trades Disputes Act in 1927 to make all future general strikes illegal. Workers could no longer come out on strike in sympathy with other workers.
- The General Strike was a disaster for the trade union movement. TUC membership fell from 5.5 million in 1925 to 3.75 million in 1930. Nevertheless, it was a success for the Labour Party. Many workers now turned away from strike action and began to support the idea of a Labour government to improve their living and working conditions. In 1929, the Labour Party, for the first time, won more seats than either the Liberals or Conservatives.

Revision tasks

1 Draw a timeline of the events of 1918–26 that led to the General Strike.

2 Use key words to explain the effects that the failure of the strike had on:
 ● the miners   ● the coal industry   ● the trade union movement
 ● the Labour Party.

3 Make a copy of the table below. Make a decision on the importance of each factor in bringing about the failure of the strike. Use information from this section to explain your decisions. An example has been done for you.

	Decisive	Important	Quite important
Government preparations			
The work of volunteers			
Government propaganda	This was decisive because it convinced the general public that the strike was wrong.		
Stanley Baldwin			
TUC mistakes			

4

SOURCE 4

An extract from Baldwin's radio broadcast of 6 May.

Constitutional government is being attacked. The laws of England are people's birthright. These laws are in your keeping. You have made Parliament their guardian. The General Strike is a challenge to Parliament, and is the road to ruin.

Look at Source 4. How reliable is this as a view of the General Strike of 1926?

Exam tip: q4 You need to evaluate:
● what is reliable about what the source shows and suggests about the General Strike compared to your knowledge of the strike
● what the limitations of the source are in what it shows and suggests, bringing in your own contextual knowledge of the General Strike
● what is reliable and unreliable about who made the broadcast and its purpose.

Key content

You need to have a good working knowledge of the following areas:
● the methods and activities of the WSPU, WFL and NUWSS
● the reaction of the Liberal Government to the women's suffrage movement
● child welfare measures, OAPs and insurance against sickness and unemployment
● the role of the BEF in 1914
● the part played by the British on the Western Front, 1915–17, especially the Battle of the Somme
● the trench system, trench warfare and new weapons
● the part played by the British in the defeat of Germany in 1918
● the role of DORA, censorship and propaganda
● recruitment and rationing
● the impact of the First World War on the position of women
● changes in the position of women in the 1920s
● the industrial unrest in the years 1918–26
● the problems of the coal industry after the First World War
● the reasons for the failure of the General Strike
● the effects of the General Strike on the coal industry and the trade union movement.

Chapter 11: War and the transformation of British society c.1931–51

During this period Britain experienced a major economic depression and became involved in the Second World War. In the years after 1945 the Labour Government introduced important changes which created the welfare state.

Key issues

As with all examination topics, you will be expected to do more than simply learn the content and write it out again. You will need to show understanding of key issues from the period. These are:

- the impact of the Depression, 1931–39
- Britain alone
- Britain at war
- Labour in power, 1945–51.

11.1 The impact of the Depression, 1931–39

The Wall Street Crash in the USA in 1929 (see Chapter 9) led to a worldwide depression. Indeed, Britain followed the USA into depression with the decline of its traditional heavy industries – coal, iron and steel, cotton and shipbuilding.

Unemployment and the government response

Unemployment reached a peak of nearly 3 million by 1933 but varied considerably from area to area.

'Depressed' Britain

In 1931, the national unemployment rate was 23 per cent, but this figure hid the real effects of the Depression. By the mid-1930s, the worst hit areas, such as Jarrow on Tyneside and Merthyr Tydfil in south Wales, had over 60 per cent unemployment. In Birmingham and Oxford, it was less than six per cent.

In Jarrow, the local coal mine, Hebburn Colliery, closed in 1930. In the following year, the steel works closed. In 1934, National Shipbuilders' Security Ltd, an organisation set up to close shipyards which were not profitable, shut down Palmer's, the shipyard in Jarrow. This had a devastating effect on the town. Ellen Wilkinson, the local Labour MP, described it as 'the town that was murdered'.

The government response

There is much debate on government action. Did it do enough to help the 'depressed areas' and the unemployed? In 1931, a National Government was set up to reduce unemployment. This was a coalition of the three main parties – Conservatives, Liberals and Labour.

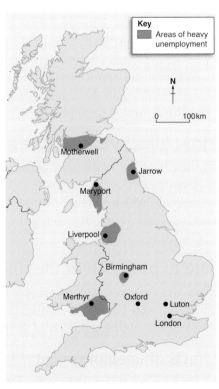

Unemployment in Britain in the 1930s.

- *Unemployment benefit.* For those out of work, there was unemployment benefit (or dole money). Between 1929 and 1931, the numbers of unemployed grew rapidly. The Government found it was paying far more out in benefits than it was receiving in taxes. As a consequence, the National Government cut unemployment benefit by ten per cent in 1931. It also introduced the means test.
- *The means test, 1931.* Many people claimed that the means test was more about the Government trying to save money than helping the unemployed. It was carried out by officials from the local authorities' Public Assistance Committees (PACs), which had been set up in 1930. The unemployed who were claiming benefit had to reveal what everyone in their house, including grown-up children, had in savings and earnings. The test even looked at the value of things in the home that could be sold to raise money. The means test was extremely unpopular.
  - It was humiliating for families to have to reveal earnings, savings and the value of things they owned.
  - If the officials thought there was enough money in the house, they would stop the dole.
  - Some local authorities applied the means test very harshly. Others, such as those in County Durham, refused to carry it out.
  - The test created great strain in families, especially if one of the older children who had a job was forced to pay more towards the family funds.
- *Import Duties Act, 1932.* The Government tried to protect British industry by increasing the price of foreign goods. The idea was that if more British goods were bought, more would have to be produced, and so more people would be employed to produce them. The Import Duties Act benefited British car and electrical goods industries in the south of England but had little effect in areas of high unemployment. Moreover, other countries put taxes on goods coming into their country from Britain. This made it more difficult for British export industries.
- *Special Areas Act, 1934.* The Government realised that certain parts of the country were suffering far more than others from the Depression. It decided to give additional help to these 'special' areas. The Special Areas Act appointed two commissioners with a budget of two million pounds to try to attract some of the new industries to the old industrial areas. The initiative had limited success. Some industrial estates were established, such as the Team Valley Trading Estate in Gateshead, but it created fewer than 15,000 jobs. Many companies did not want to move to the north of England. Small industrial estates could not replace the coal mining or shipbuilding industries.

Exam tip Remember to give a balanced view of government measures. Some helped and some hindered the plight of the unemployed.

How effective were these measures?

By the end of the 1930s unemployment had fallen to 1 million. This was due partly to government policies and partly to favourable circumstances such as a revival in world trade, which helped Britain's exports. It was also due to rearmament, which greatly helped the traditional industries, especially coal, iron and steel, and shipbuilding.

The experience of the unemployed

In an area of high unemployment, everyone in the community felt the impact when jobs were lost. Local shopkeepers were hit hard. Shops closed, with the shopkeepers joining the ranks of the unemployed.

Effects of unemployment

- **Poverty**. Several surveys of the 1930s showed the connection between unemployment and poverty. In 1936, Seebohm Rowntree did a survey of

Comment

Some historians have argued that the measures undertaken by the National Government actually made the situation worse. They point to the means test and Import Duties Act as examples. The latter encouraged other countries to put duties on British goods and made it more difficult to export.

poverty in York and found that 72.6 per cent of unemployed workers lived below the poverty line.

- **Health**. Not surprisingly, the health of the unemployed and their families, especially children, suffered. Several studies showed that the unemployed had an inadequate diet. They ate a lot of bread, margarine, potatoes, sugar and tea, but little meat, fresh fruit and vegetables, and milk.
- **Psychological**. One common consequence of unemployment was poor mental health. Investigators found a general trend. The first week or so of unemployment was treated as a holiday. People got up early, put on their best clothes and went down to their local labour exchange seeking work. After a few weeks, confidence began to decline, expectations fell and the unemployed took less interest in personal appearance. Many people, used to being the breadwinner of the family, felt guilty and lost all self-respect and self-esteem.

Revision tasks

1 Make a copy of the table below. Use the information in this section to explain each measure and whether it helped or hindered Britain's economic position.

Measure	Explanation	Help	Hinder
Unemployment benefit			
Means test			
Import Duties Act			
Special Areas Act			

2 What effects did the Depression have on the standard of living of the unemployed?

The Jarrow Crusade

This is one of the most famous events of the 1930s.

Reasons for march

Palmer's shipyard in Jarrow began to decline after the First World War. There were fewer warships being built and after 1929 fewer and fewer cargo ships. In the early 1930s orders dried up completely. Unemployment rose from 3,245 in 1929 to 7,178 in 1933.

The end came in 1934. A group of shipyard owners set up National Shipbuilders' Security Ltd (see page 113). They decided to buy up smaller yards and then scrap them. Palmer's was one of the first to go. In 1934 it was bought up and the yard was closed. It was announced that no ships would be built there for 40 years. This had a terrible effect on Jarrow. Unemployment reached 80 per cent at one point.

The march

The people of Jarrow decided to fight back. Public meetings were held and the town council decided to draw up a petition demanding the right to work. It organised a march to London to present the petition to the Government. Two hundred men were carefully selected by the local officer of health for the long journey to London. The men decided to march between 15 and 25 miles per day.

There had been a number of hunger marches previously, but the Jarrow march caught the public imagination. It had been approved by the local council and the marchers were led on their journey by Ellen Wilkinson MP. Each night the marchers were accommodated along the route by householders who supported their cause. The press gave the protestors mouth organs so they could march to music.

Comment

Palmer's also suffered from another problem. By the 1930s the yard was too small for the type of ship that was being built. The Queen Elizabeth *and* Queen Mary, *which were launched in the 1930s, were over 80,000 tonnes. Palmer's could not cope with ships that size.*

What it achieved

- It publicised the plight of towns like Jarrow to people in the more prosperous south of England.
- The police praised the marchers for being well organised and disciplined.
- The men returned home as heroes.
- A few men found work in the Team Valley Trading Estate in nearby Gateshead.

However:

- The Government refused to let them present the petition when they got to London.
- They did not get new work for the town.
- When they returned to Jarrow, they discovered that their unemployment benefit had been stopped as they had not been available for work while on the march.

Exam tip Students often write that the Jarrow march was a total success. Remember, it did little to bring employment to Jarrow.

Revision tasks

1 Make a copy of the set of scales shown here. Use key words to complete each side of the scales.

2 Was the Jarrow march a success? Explain your answer.

Achievements of the Jarrow march | Failures of the Jarrow march

3

SOURCE 1

From *Love on the Dole*, a novel written by Walter Greenwood in the 1930s.

It got to you slowly like a malignant disease. You fell into the habit of slouching, of putting your hands in your pockets and keeping them there. Of glancing at people secretly, ashamed of your secret. You prayed for the winter evenings and the kindly darkness. Pants with the backside patched and re-patched; patches on knees, on elbows. Jesus! All bloody patches.

What can you learn from Source 1 about the effects of unemployment?

Exam tip: q3 This is a Unit 3 inference question. An inference means what the source is suggesting; what messages it is giving.
- You need to make at least two inferences.
- Support each inference with evidence from the source.

11.2 Britain alone

Britain entered the Second World War in September 1939. By June 1940 France had been defeated and Britain alone faced Germany and Italy from 1940 to 1941 until the German invasion of the USSR.

The British Expeditionary Force, Dunkirk and Churchill

Hitler's armies invaded and defeated Poland in September 1939.

The British Expeditionary Force

From the end of September 1939 to April 1940, little progress was made in the war in the west. This became known as the 'Phoney War' (or pretend war) in Britain and the *Sitzkrieg*, or sitting war, in Germany.

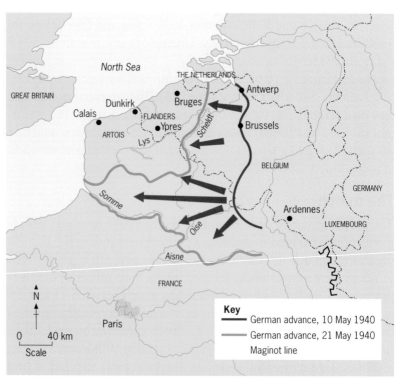

The German advance through Belgium and France, May 1940.

The defeat of France

On 13 May 1940, the Germans launched a *Blitzkrieg* attack against the Low Countries (Belgium and the Netherlands) and France. It was an outstanding success. German attacks rolled swiftly across the Netherlands and Belgium. Dutch attempts to delay the German advances by opening the dykes and flooding the land were too little too late. The Germans used glider planes to land behind the Belgian lines of defences and outflank their defenders. The Netherlands surrendered within five days.

Other troops attacked the French. The French High Command was sure that the expensive line of underground forts on the **Maginot Line** would stop any German attack. The Germans, however, decided not to attack this line – *Blitzkrieg* avoided enemy strongpoints. Instead the Germans attacked the weakest part of the French defences, the Ardennes. This was a heavily wooded area, which seemed unsuitable for tanks. To the astonishment of the French, the Germans attacked this area and broke through to Sedan.

French resistance crumbled as the German tanks raced through to the Channel coast, where they planned to cut off the retreat of the 200,000-strong BEF. By the tenth day, the Germans had reached the Channel. Eight days later, Belgium surrendered.

Key terms

Maginot Line: a line of fortifications along the north east frontier of France.

Dunkirk

British and French troops retreated to Dunkirk where they awaited either evacuation or capture. For reasons that are not quite clear, Hitler ordered the advancing German troops to stop. This gave the Allies a breathing space in which to carry out an evacuation. Between 26 May and 4 June 198,000 British and 140,000 French and Belgian troops were evacuated.

Dunkirk was celebrated in Britain as a great achievement.
- The RAF outfought the Luftwaffe (the German air force) over the beaches of Dunkirk. It was a great success for the British navy.
- Many troops were rescued to fight another day.
- The 'Dunkirk spirit' was born. Winston Churchill, the Prime Minister, made the British determined to fight against Hitler.

However, in many respects it was a disaster.
- Around 300,000 troops were left behind and forced to surrender.
- Most of the army's equipment had to be abandoned.
- France was left to fight alone and soon surrendered.

Within a month of the Dunkirk evacuation, Paris had been captured and France had surrendered to Germany. Instead of occupying the whole of France, Germany allowed southern France to set up a government at Vichy run by General Petain. The Vichy Government was really controlled by the Germans.

Comment

Churchill portrayed Dunkirk as a great British victory due to the evacuation of so many troops. This was, in most respects, government propaganda to keep up the morale of the British people.

Exam tip Ensure you give a balanced view of Dunkirk.

Churchill

One of the main reasons for British survival in the years 1940–41 was the leadership of Winston Churchill, who had replaced Neville Chamberlain as Prime Minister in May 1940.
- He immediately brought a new urgency to the war effort. He helped to create the 'Dunkirk spirit', turning a defeat into an apparent success for the British. He insisted that Britain would never surrender and built up the confidence and morale of the British people through his speeches and 'bulldog' approach.
- Churchill also cultivated close relations with the USA and its president, Roosevelt. Although the USA remained neutral, Roosevelt was prepared to supply Britain with the needs of war, through an agreement called 'Lend Lease'. These supplies proved vital during this difficult period.

Comment

Churchill and the spirit of the British people are rightly praised for Britain's survival alone against Germany between 1940 and 1941. Yet Britain's survival was also due to favourable circumstances, such as Hitler's decision not to use tanks at Dunkirk, Roosevelt's willingness to agree to Lend Lease and, most important of all, Hitler's decision to invade the Soviet Union in June 1941.

Revision task

Make a copy of the table below. Use information from this section to give your verdict on Dunkirk – success or disaster.

Success	Disaster

The Battle of Britain

One of the most important reasons for British survival in the war was the defeat of the German air force during the Battle of Britain.

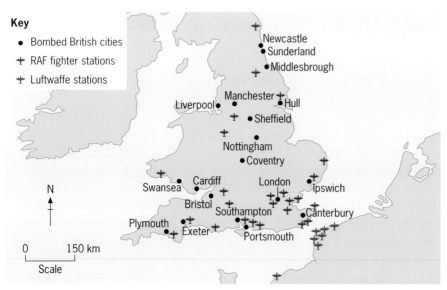

Key
- Bombed British cities
- + RAF fighter stations
- + Luftwaffe stations

The Battle of Britain.

Britain would not have survived without the RAF and its successes in the Battle of Britain. Hitler planned to attack Britain but first he needed to destroy the RAF and gain control of the skies over Britain. The first attacks by the German Luftwaffe were on shipping in the English Channel and the ports on the south coast. These were followed by bombing raids on radar stations and then airfields. Finally, from mid-August, came the attacks on Fighter Command. By the first week in September the Luftwaffe were getting the upper hand as the RAF ran out of reserves of pilots and planes. Fortunately Hitler diverted the Luftwaffe to attacks on London. When daylight raids were renewed on 15 September, the RAF regained the initiative.

The RAF was successful for several reasons:
- German mistakes – Hitler made the mistake of diverting the Luftwaffe from attacks on the RAF to bombing London.
- German weaknesses – the German bombers were often not escorted by fighter planes. They became easy targets for the RAF fighters.
- The British had superior fighter planes – the Spitfire and the Hurricane.
- Since the mid-1930s the British had devised an early warning system using radar which meant they knew when and where the Germans would attack. RAF fighter planes were in the air and ready when the German bombers and fighters appeared.

The Blitz

This was the name given to German attempts to bomb Britain out of the war.

German bombing

The Luftwaffe's bombing of British towns and cities became known as the 'Blitz'. Hitler hoped that the Blitz would force Britain to surrender and that the German people would enjoy revenge for the bombing that they had suffered. (On 25 August 1940, Britain had begun the night-bombing of German towns and cities.) From 7 September until 2 November 1940, London was bombed every night. Bombs landed on London Zoo and the papers reported that 'the morale of the monkeys remained unaffected'. The House of Commons building was destroyed and the Commons had to move into the House of Lords. Buckingham Palace was damaged but King George VI was often on the scene after a severe raid to encourage people as they struggled to save those trapped under the debris.

The German bombing raids continued until well into 1941, when most of the Luftwaffe was needed on the Eastern Front. London was not the only city to suffer. The Germans also attacked other towns and cities such as Hull, Plymouth, Bristol, Liverpool, Manchester and Birmingham. The most famous of these attacks was the raid on Coventry. On the night of 14 November 1940, much of the city, including the cathedral, was destroyed. Yet in spite of this savage raid, the factories in Coventry were back in full production within five days.

Other smaller towns and cities were hit in 1941–42 in the so-called Baedeker raids. The targets were chosen by the Germans from the Baedeker tourist guide book. The cathedral cities of Canterbury and Norwich were among those hit.

There were further air attacks in 1944–45 from V-1 and V-2 missiles, based in northern France.

- Six thousand V-1 bombs reached targets in Britain, causing 20,000 casualties and considerable damage to houses.
- Around 500 V-2s hit London between September 1944 and March 1945, causing 9,000 casualties.

Air raid precautions

The Government supplied its citizens with air raid shelters.

- The first shelters were delivered in February 1939. These were Anderson shelters, which were sunk into the ground in people's gardens. They had enough room for a family and were safer than staying in a house.
- Later, in 1941, the Morrison shelter was introduced, which could be erected indoors. By the end of the year 500,000 of these shelters had been distributed.

When the raids first began, people in London were not allowed to use the underground railway stations for fear they would get trapped. But public pressure forced the authorities to give way and they became popular places to shelter.

The 'blackout' had the most immediate effect on the British people. In order that German bombers would not see cities from the air, and therefore target their bombing more precisely, people had to ensure that no light was visible from their homes. Failure to do so meant a visit from the Air Raid Warden. Streetlights were not lit and cars had to drive without lights. This led to many accidents. In December 1939, over 1,500 people were killed on British roads. This was nearly three times the pre-war average of 600 deaths per month.

Evacuation

The Government expected that the Germans would attack Britain from the air so it took precautions to protect its civilians from bombings and gas attacks. Children were protected by being moved (evacuated) from the likeliest targets, the cities, into the countryside. The first evacuation was announced on 31 August 1939, the day before Hitler invaded Poland.

Many parents were reluctant to be separated from their children but did accept that they would be safer. Parents were told what the children needed to take with them and where they were to assemble for evacuation. The evacuation began on 1 September 1939. Many city schools were closed and many teachers went with the children to the countryside to continue teaching them.

At their destinations, the evacuees gathered in village or school halls where they were chosen by the foster family they were to live with. Homesickness and the 'Phoney War' (see page 116) saw many children drift back to the cities by Christmas 1939. When German planes started bombing London in 1940, a second evacuation from the cities took place, although not on the scale of the evacuation of 1939.

Was evacuation a success?

Successes	Criticisms
<ul><li>Some children were very happy. They helped on farms and had far better diets than they had done before.</li><li>Thousands were moved to the safety of the countryside and away from the bombing.</li><li>In the long term, evacuation encouraged further social reform as it highlighted the poor condition of many children from the inner cities.</li><li>It enabled mothers to take on vital war work.</li></ul>	<ul><li>Many mothers and children returned to their homes during the 'Phoney War' and had to be evacuated again.</li><li>The administration of evacuees was often chaotic with a mismatch in numbers of evacuees and foster homes.</li><li>Some children had a miserable time. They were resented as a burden by their foster families, and they missed their own families, far away in the cities.</li><li>Many country families were shocked by the evacuees they looked after. They had to deal with children who wet their beds and had no experience of using a knife and fork.</li></ul>

Revision tasks

1 Make a copy of these concentric circles. Write a reason in each circle for British success in the Battle of Britain, beginning with the most important in the middle. Use key words to explain your decisions.

2 Complete a table for the Blitz, like the one below, listing the successes and failures of this tactic from the German point of view.

Successes	Failures

3 Use key words to explain how the following were affected by evacuation:
   • mothers   • children   • country families.

4

SOURCE 2   A British poster from 1940.

"NEVER WAS SO MUCH OWED BY SO MANY TO SO FEW" *THE PRIME MINISTER*

What was the purpose of Source 2? Explain your answer using details from the source and your own knowledge.

Exam tip: q4 You need to explain:
• what the source is suggesting
• what message it is trying to get across
• what its purpose is. What is it trying to make people think or do?

11.3 Britain at war

The role of the Government and women changed during the Second World War.

The role of government

The Government was responsible for propaganda and censorship as well as introducing rationing due to food shortages.

Propaganda

The Ministry of Information was responsible for propaganda and censorship. It monitored public opinion through an organisation called Mass Observation, which carried out surveys and reported on conversations in shops and pubs.

Propaganda was used in several ways.

- Poster campaigns encouraged people to join the voluntary services and work hard in order to help the war effort.
- Posters also warned people of the dangers of 'careless talk'. There was a fear that German spies could be working in the country so people were told not to discuss the war in public.
- Posters encouraged people to save for the war effort and not to waste food and other resources. The 'squander bug' became a regular feature of messages to housewives.

Censorship

Newspapers were censored by the Government during the war. They reported on the bombings but in an attempt to keep up morale they concentrated on the heroism of the rescuers rather than the deaths and injuries. The Government banned the publication of the *Daily Worker* newspaper in 1941 when it claimed that the war was being fought for the benefit of the bosses.

Rationing

At the outbreak of war, Britain grew only enough food to feed about one person in every three. Much food was imported but, as with the First World War, these imports were threatened by the activities of the German U-boats.

The Government introduced a series of measures to ensure there was an adequate supply of food. Rationing was introduced as early as January 1940. Each person had a ration book filled with coupons, which they used to buy the amount of food they were entitled to each week. Later, a points system was introduced, to give people greater choice in what they could buy. The Board of Trade also issued recipes showing people how to make healthy meals using food that was available.

At first, only butter, bacon and sugar were rationed. Later, this was extended to include tea and most basic foodstuffs, although vegetables were never rationed. People were asked to grow their own food so that less food would have to be imported. Window boxes, lawns, public parks and golf courses were used to grow vegetables to keep the nation fed and healthy.

> ### Revision tasks
> 1 Why was it necessary to introduce rationing?
> 2 Draw a spider diagram to show government measures in connection with rationing.

The changing role of women

Women's work

Industry was short of workers as men were conscripted. At first, women volunteered to fill vacant jobs. By 1941, industry was so short of workers that unmarried women were conscripted. Within two years, 57 per cent of workers were female. By 1943, nine out of ten single women were doing war work, and so were many married women. Some worked in industry, and those who worked in dangerous conditions, such as in the munitions industry, were well paid. Men were usually better paid for doing the same jobs but, even so, women were earning a lot more than before the war.

There was a similar shortage of workers on the land. About 80,000 women joined the Women's Land Army. They were given lodgings in remote areas, sometimes with very basic conditions. Many women travelled the country doing everyday farm jobs, such as haymaking, ploughing, harvesting and looking after animals.

Women in the armed forces

Women who were conscripted after 1941 could choose to join one of three organisations:
- the Auxiliary Territorial Service (ATS)
- the Women's Auxiliary Air Force (WAAF)
- the Women's Royal Naval Service (WRNS).

These forces were involved in providing support services rather than fighting, but they worked alongside men and faced the same dangers. Women operated searchlights or acted as radar controllers. Women pilots were also used to transfer planes from the factories to the airfields.

Effects on women

Life for many women had been very strict during the 1930s, but in wartime, there was a shortage of younger men at home, and there tended to be more freedom in sexual relationships. Some women argued that with all the dangers and worries of wartime they should be allowed to enjoy themselves.

But equality was still far off. For example, the Government would not commit itself to equal pay for women. An Equal Pay Commission was set up in 1943 and reported in 1946, but it had no powers to make recommendations. Similarly, the Ministry of Health refused to set up nurseries to provide childcare for working women, arguing that female employment was only for the duration of the war. By 1944 there were, however, 1,450 nurseries compared to 104 before the war. These were closed down after the war to force married women to give up their jobs and return to the home.

When the war ended, fewer women wanted to work. Many saw work as a wartime emergency and believed that their proper place was in the home. Many had delayed having children because of the war and now wanted to start families. The war did, however, bring some changes in attitudes towards married women working. In the 1950s, some of these women did find work when their children were growing up.

Comment

By 1944, there were 450,000 women working in these three armed services. Many women worked as mechanics, welders, carpenters and even gunners on anti-aircraft guns. However, traditional attitudes towards women remained. Most women in the services worked as cooks, cleaners or secretaries.

Comment

Women played a very important role on the Home Front but, as with the First World War, made limited gains in terms of job opportunities and their social position. After the war, most were expected to give up their jobs and return to their pre-war employment or settle for marriage and the roles of mother and housewife.

Revision task

SOURCE 3 — A poster issued by the British Government during the Second World War.

How useful is Source 3 as evidence of the work of women during the Second World War?

Exam tip You need to evaluate:
- what is useful about the source and what it suggests about the work of women
- the limitations of what it shows and suggests, bringing in your own contextual knowledge of the work of women
- what is useful and what are the limitations of the purpose of the poster; of why it was used.

D-Day and the defeat of Germany

The British played an important role in the D-Day invasions of 1944 and the eventual defeat of Germany.

D-Day

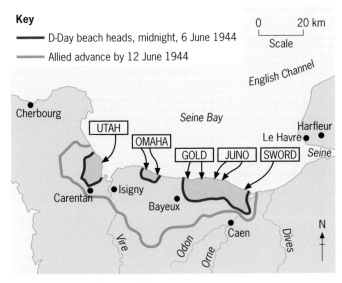

D-Day landings, June 1944.

On 6 June 1944 Allied forces landed on the beaches of Normandy in France and began the campaign to liberate western Europe from German occupation. The British and Canadian forces landed on beaches codenamed Sword, Juno and Gold and the US forces landed at Omaha and Utah. The Allies were quickly able to establish a beachhead (or fortified position) and, although pinned down in Normandy for almost a month, they eventually broke out and reached Paris within six weeks.

The success of D-Day was due to a combination of factors:
- The Allies had prepared very thoroughly for the invasion. Churchill delayed the assault until he felt the time was right. Allied troops were trained in landing tactics and new devices were developed to assist in the landings. These included artificial piers and harbours and an oil pipeline across the Channel.
- The Germans did not know where the landings would take place. Indeed, Allied bombing of the Calais area convinced Hitler that this would be the location. Even on the day of the invasion, he thought the landings in Normandy were a decoy and was slow to send reinforcements.
- The Allies had control of the air over the Channel and northern France. Ten thousand Allied planes escorted the invasion fleet and had also prepared the way by bombing communications to Normandy and carrying paratroopers behind German lines. The invasion fleet was the biggest ever assembled.
- Hitler refused to allow Field Marshal Rommel to take control of the Panzer tank divisions in Normandy. This weakened the German army when it tried to counter-attack the Allies after they had landed.

The defeat of Germany

It took a further eleven months after D-Day to defeat the Germans. This delay was due to the following factors:
- The Americans decided to advance slowly on a broad front rather than make a concentrated strike at the Germans, which might overstretch supply lines and risk Allied forces being cut off by a German counter-attack. The British did attempt to speed up the advance through the Arnhem operation of September

1944. Airborne troops were landed behind the German lines in the Netherlands in an attempt to outflank the German defences. The plan failed because the land troops were unable to link up with the paratroopers.

- Hitler took a final gamble on victory in December 1944, in an attack known as the Battle of the Bulge. He tried to repeat the success of the Ardennes operation of 1940 when the German armies successfully broke through the French defences, but this time against the Americans. American troops were taken by surprise and the Germans only narrowly failed to achieve a breakthrough. It took the Americans nearly two months to recover the area they had lost in the offensive.

In March 1945 Allied troops finally crossed the Rhine and moved into Germany. By this time Germany was on its knees, having been bombed around the clock and starved by the Allied naval blockade. The surrender was signed in northern Germany on 8 May 1945.

Although the Allied landings in Normandy and their subsequent advance played an important role in the defeat of Germany, the crucial area was probably the Eastern Front. It was in the Soviet Union that the German army had 90 per cent of its casualties.

Revision tasks

1 Make a copy of the following table about women and the war. Use key words to complete each column.

Key areas	Explanation
Industry	
Land Army	
Armed forces	

2 Did women improve their position as a result of their role on the Home Front? Draw up a balance sheet to illustrate your answer, showing progress and lack of progress.

3 Make a copy of the table below. Complete it using the information from this section to explain the events of 1944–45.

Event	Explanation
Preparations for D-Day	
D-Day landings	
Allied advance	
Why the Allied advance slowed down	

4 Using information from this section, make a list of reasons for the success of the landings on D-Day.

11.4 Labour in power, 1945–51

Labour won the general election of 1945 and introduced a series of reforms including the National Health Service.

Labour comes to power

The 1945 general election produced a massive landslide victory for the Labour Party, with Labour winning 393 seats to the 213 of the Conservatives. The victory was due to the unpopularity of the Conservatives and the appeal of Labour.

Unpopularity of Conservatives	Appeal of Labour
• Churchill's popularity as a wartime leader did not carry over to peacetime. Many, especially in the working class, remembered his attitude during the General Strike of 1926 when he showed no sympathy for the miners. His comment that a Labour government might have to fall back on 'some sort of Gestapo' did not go down well. • The Conservative Party was associated with the grim economic depression of the 1930s and with the policy of appeasement which failed to prevent the outbreak of the Second World War. • The Conservatives stated that they accepted all of the proposals of the Beveridge Report (see below), but that putting them into practice immediately would be very difficult. Winston Churchill, in an unguarded moment, said he opposed the idea of a welfare state. This made many people vote for Labour.	• In 1945 there was a powerful feeling in Britain in favour of reform – for widespread economic and social changes – encouraged by the sacrifices of the Second World War and the Beveridge Report. This would not be provided by the tired Conservative Party. • The Labour leader, Clement Attlee, struck just the right note with the electorate of calm assurance and confidence. Moreover, Attlee and other Labour leaders had played a crucial role in the Churchill wartime Government. Morrison, Bevin and Cripps were now household names. • Labour seemed to be the party promising change and was not associated with the mistakes of the 1930s. It was judged as best fitted to undertake the task of reconstruction and reform.

Responding to Beveridge: the attack on want

The Labour Government of 1945–51 welcomed the Beveridge Report of 1942.

The Beveridge Report

In 1941, the Government asked Sir William Beveridge to suggest ways in which it could help the sick, the unemployed, low-paid workers and retired people. Beveridge produced his report in 1942. He identified five giant problems that had to be overcome to make progress and create a better society.

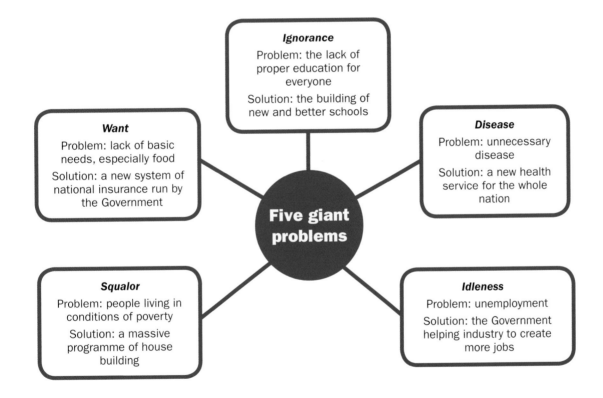

The attack on want

Labour followed most of the recommendations of the Beveridge Report to try to reduce poverty.

- *Family allowances.* To improve the standard of living, the idea of a family allowance was introduced in 1945 and the first payments were made in August 1946. A family received five shillings (25p) a week for each child after the first until each child reached the age of sixteen or was employed full time. There was no means test – all families received the benefit.
- *National Insurance.* The National Insurance Act was introduced in 1946.
  - Employers, workers and the Government all paid into the scheme.
  - It provided benefits to workers who were out of work due to sickness, unemployment or pregnancy.
  - There was no limit to how long a person could claim sickness benefit.
  - The unemployed could claim unemployment benefit for only six months.
- *National Insurance (Industrial Injuries) Act, 1946.* This act gave benefits to workers who were injured or disabled while at work and set up tribunals (courts) to decide the amount of compensation to be paid.
- *National Assistance Act, 1948.* Two years later, Labour passed the National Assistance Act to provide for those in great need, especially those not covered by the National Insurance Act. It set up a board whose purpose was to prevent extreme poverty and provide everyone with a minimum income. *The Times* newspaper said that the National Assistance Board was now 'the citizen's last defence against extreme poverty'.

The National Health Service

Aneurin Bevan, the Minister for Health, was responsible for improving the nation's health. In 1946, he introduced the National Health Service Act.

Attack on disease

- Everyone received free medical, dental, hospital and eye treatment.
- There was no charge for spectacles, false teeth or medicines.
- Most hospitals came under government control as part of the National Health Service (NHS).
- Local councils provided midwives, home nurses, health visitors and ambulances.
- All these services were paid for by taxation and National Insurance contributions.
- Doctors were paid under the NHS, which encouraged general practitioners (GPs) to practise in poorer areas without the fear of going unpaid because people could not afford the fees.

The NHS was fiercely opposed by the medical profession. By January 1948, only one in every 100 specialist doctors and surgeons in London was in favour of the scheme. They argued that they would lose their independence, spend valuable time filling in forms and have their earnings controlled by the Government. Bevan had to give way to the British Medical Association (BMA), which represented the doctors. He allowed them to treat private patients and gave them a guaranteed income each year – not just a payment each time they treated a patient. The opposition collapsed and the NHS came into being on 5 July 1948.

The importance of the NHS

The NHS brought many benefits, such as:

- improvements in medical care, such as a fall in the infant mortality rate
- better provision for older people, such as false teeth, good-quality spectacles and efficient hearing aids

- free ante-natal clinics and maternity benefit for mothers
- a reduction in deaths from diseases such as tuberculosis and diphtheria
- dental treatment for 8.5 million people and spectacles for 5.25 million people in the first year alone.

However, it also brought problems.
- The NHS was very expensive to run. It cost £400 million in its first year.
- Others said that it encouraged people who wanted something for nothing and that taxpayers' money was being needlessly squandered.
- Some disliked the fact that there was still private practice. They argued that this would lead to twin standards and better care for those who could afford to pay.
- In 1951, the Labour Government introduced charges for spectacles, false teeth and prescriptions. Bevan resigned in protest, insisting that everything should be free.

Comment

Many of the measures introduced by the Labour Government were not new. For example, National Insurance built on the work of previous governments, especially the Liberals. The National Health Service was new though, and it showed the commitment of the Labour Party to the creation of a welfare state.

Revision tasks

1 Draw a mind map showing the reasons for the Labour election victory of 1945. Put the reasons in order, clockwise, beginning with the most important at twelve o'clock.

2 Why was the Beveridge Report so important?

3 Make a copy of the table below. Use the information from this section to explain the measures introduced to attack want.

Measure	Explanation
Family allowance	
National Insurance	
National Insurance (Industrial Injuries)	
National Assistance	

4 Draw up a balance sheet for the NHS. Was the NHS a great success?

5

SOURCE 4

An 83-year-old woman, interviewed in 1998, remembers the start of the National Health Service.

When the National Health Service came in it was much easier to see a doctor, and it was free! My teeth had been bad since I had a baby and I was now able to have false teeth at no cost. They were sore at first but soon bedded in and became comfortable. Some of my friends got teeth because they were free but never used them. My mum got free spectacles and we all noticed how much better she could see.

How reliable is Source 4 as a view of the beginning of the National Health Service?

Exam tip: q5 You need to evaluate:
- what is reliable about what the source suggests about the NHS compared to your knowledge of the beginning of the NHS
- what the limitations are of what the source suggests, bringing in your own contextual knowledge of the beginning of the NHS
- what is reliable and unreliable about who gave the interview, when it was given and its purpose.

Key content

You need to have a good working knowledge of the following areas:

- the impact of the Depression 1931–39, including the growth of unemployment
- government measures to deal with unemployment
- the experience of the unemployed and the importance of the Jarrow Crusade
- the part played by the BEF, 1939–40, and the defeat of France
- the achievements and shortcomings of Dunkirk
- the importance of Churchill's leadership, 1940–41
- the importance of the Battle of Britain and the reasons for British victory
- the impact of the Blitz on Britain
- air raid shelters, the blackout and evacuation
- rationing, censorship and propaganda
- the changing role of women during the Second World War
- the D-Day landings and the defeat of Germany
- reasons for the Labour election victory of 1945
- the importance of the Beveridge Report
- the attack on want
- the setting up and immediate achievements of the NHS.

The Second World War greatly benefited the USA, which emerged as the leading economy of the world. There were, however, many tensions within US society during the war which later led to great unrest and upheaval and in particular to the movements for civil rights. The USA was also greatly divided by McCarthyism and the fear of Communism, and by the students' and women's movements of the 1960s.

Key issues

As with all examination topics, you will be expected to do more than simply learn the content and write it out again. You will need to show understanding of key issues from the period. These are:

- McCarthyism and the Red Scare
- the civil rights movement, 1945–62
- changes in the civil rights movement, 1963–70
- other protest movements of the 1960s.

12.1 McCarthyism and the Red Scare

In the years after 1945 the USA experienced a 'Red Scare' which led to a movement known as McCarthyism.

The impact of the Cold War

One major reason for the development of the Red Scare in the USA was the early **Cold War** between the USA and the Soviet Union.

The early Cold War

The USA and the Soviet Union had been reluctant allies during the Second World War against Hitler and Germany because of the clash between capitalism and Communism. Harry Truman, who became President of the USA in early 1945, did not think that the USSR could be trusted and his advisers urged him to 'get tough' with Stalin. At the Potsdam Conference in July 1945, Truman knew that the atomic bomb had been successfully tested and, in the words of Churchill, 'he generally bossed the whole meeting'. After the war, Truman felt that the alliance with the Soviet Union was less important. (See Chapter 4 for more information on the Cold War.)

Soviet expansion

Truman's suspicions about Stalin increased due to Soviet expansion into eastern Europe in the years immediately following the Second World War, more especially Poland, Czechoslovakia, Hungary, Romania and Bulgaria. The USA was determined to contain further expansion into western Europe.

Key terms

Cold War: A 'stand off' or a war of nerves between the USA and the USSR.

US containment

Truman responded to Soviet expansion by announcing the Truman **Doctrine** in 1947, under which the USA was committed to supporting all nations that were threatened with a Communist takeover. This was followed immediately by Marshall Aid, which committed America to providing economic aid to countries in western Europe which had suffered from the effects of the Second World War. American aid would encourage economic recovery and prevent a possible Communist takeover.

Events 1948–50

The growing fear of Communism was intensified by the Berlin crisis of 1948–49 (see page 43), the first Cold War crisis. The Berlin **blockade** showed that Stalin was prepared to risk war in the hope of removing the Allies from Berlin when he stopped all land transport into the city. These events, and the Soviet development of the atom bomb, convinced the Americans that Stalin wanted world domination.

As far as Truman and his advisers were concerned, the spread of Communism had to be halted. Western countries formed the North Atlantic Treaty Organisation (NATO), which stated that an attack on any NATO member was seen as an attack on the whole alliance. The 'Cold War' was now being waged between the two superpowers.

Moreover, the success of the Communist Party in China in 1949 indicated the 'danger' of Communism as a truly worldwide threat. This seemed to be confirmed by the invasion of South Korea by the Communist North in 1950, which instigated US involvement in the Korean War.

World events had woken up many Americans to the threat of Communism, a threat which seemed greater when, in 1949, the USSR tested its first atomic bomb, several years earlier than expected.

Key terms

Doctrine: a statement of ideas.
Blockade: the surrounding of a place with troops or ships to prevent the entry or exit of supplies.

The development of the Red Scare

This fear of Communism was intensified by developments within the USA.

The Federal Bureau of Investigation and the House Un-American Activities Committee

- The Federal Bureau of Investigation (FBI) had a strongly anti-Communist director, J. Edgar Hoover. In 1947, under the Federal Employee Loyalty Program set up by President Truman, the FBI investigated government employees to see if they were current or former members of the Communist Party. From 1947 to 1950 around 3 million people were investigated. Nobody was charged for spying.
- From the 1930s, the US Congress had a House Un-American Activities Committee (HUAC), which had the right to investigate anyone suspected of doing anything un-American. 'Un-American' mostly meant Communism. In 1947 HUAC became big news. The FBI had evidence that a number of prominent Hollywood writers, producers and directors were members of the Communist Party. The so-called 'Hollywood Ten' were brought before the HUAC. They were doing nothing illegal as they were not government employees and they refused to answer questions, pleading the First Amendment. They were jailed for one year for contempt of court and 'blacklisted'. All this made front-page news.

Hiss and the Rosenbergs

- In 1948 a man called Whittaker Chambers faced the HUAC and admitted being a Communist. He also said that Alger Hiss, a high-ranking member of the US State Department, was a Communist. Hiss denied this and said he did not know Chambers. President Truman dismissed the case. Richard Nixon, a young member of HUAC, investigated further and showed that Hiss had known Chambers. In 1950 Hiss was imprisoned for five years for perjury.

- In 1951 Julius and Ethel Rosenberg were found guilty of spying for the USSR and passing on atomic secrets. Two years later they were executed. The evidence against the Rosenbergs was flimsy, although coded telegrams between the Rosenbergs and Soviet agents were later discovered.

Exam tip Be aware of events outside the USA, especially the Cold War, as well as developments in America.

The impact of McCarthyism

In 1950 Joseph McCarthy was a young Republican senator in search of a headline. He decided to take advantage of the anti-Communist hysteria that was building up in the USA.

The methods he used

- He claimed, using FBI loyalty board investigations, that he had a list of over 200 Communists in the State Department.
- This brought widespread publicity. Democrat Senator Millard Tydings declared that the charges lacked foundation. McCarthy accused Tydings of being a Communist.

In the 1952 elections the Republicans did very well, winning many seats. Tydings lost his seat to a supporter of McCarthy.

- As chairman of a Senate committee, McCarthy began to investigate Communist activities in the Government. Throughout 1952 and 1953, McCarthy extended his investigations and turned his committee into a weapon to increase his personal power. He targeted high-profile figures and accused them of Communist activities.
- Thousands of lives were ruined by McCarthy's witch-hunt. False accusations led to people being blacklisted, which meant they could not find work. Over 100 university lecturers were fired due to McCarthy, and 324 Hollywood personalities were blacklisted.

> # Comment
> *One of the accused was General George Marshall who had been responsible for the Marshall Plan of 1947. Marshall was accused of being at the centre of a gigantic Communist conspiracy against the USA.*

Exam tip Have a clear knowledge of the methods used by McCarthy.

The end of McCarthyism

McCarthyism ended in 1954 for several reasons.

- There was much influential opposition to McCarthy's activities. Many senators and some top Hollywood stars spoke up against his activities. Quality newspapers such as the *Washington Post* and *New York Times* produced reports which seriously challenged McCarthy's activities.
- In 1954 McCarthy went too far. He accused 45 army officers of being Communist agents. The hearings that followed were televised. McCarthy was rude, abusive and had a bullying manner. In contrast, the army's attorney, Joseph Welch, was polite and humiliated McCarthy. McCarthy's popularity fell dramatically. He had become an alcoholic and died three years later.

McCarthyism was important for several reasons.

- It showed the extent of anti-Communist feeling in America.
- It brought great suffering to those accused of anti-Communist activities and sympathies.
- It showed that many Americans wanted to return to the traditional values that had been disrupted by the chaos of the 1920s and 1930s and then the war years. Supporters of McCarthy would have liked women to stay in the home, African Americans to be content with their lowly place in society, and all rock and roll music to be banned.

Revision tasks

1 Make a copy of the table below on McCarthyism. Use the information from this section to complete it.

Reasons for McCarthyism	Key features of McCarthyism	Reasons why it died out	Importance of McCarthyism

2

SOURCE 1

Harry S. Truman speaking on the radio, 17 November 1953, about his views on McCarthyism.

McCarthyism … the meaning of the word is the corruption of the truth, the abandonment of our historical devotion to fair play. It is the abandonment of 'due process' of law. It is the use of the big lie and the unfounded accusation against any citizen in the name of Americanism and security … This horrible cancer is eating at the vitals of America and it can destroy the great edifice of freedom.

What can you learn from Source 1 about McCarthyism?

Exam tip: q2 This is a Unit 3 inference question. An inference means what the source is suggesting, what messages it is giving.
- You need to make at least two inferences.
- Support each inference with evidence from the source.

12.2 The civil rights movement, 1945–62

The impact of the Second World War

African Americans made a major contribution to the US war effort but still faced prejudice and discrimination in the armed forces.
- African American soldiers usually served in African-American-only units with white officers.
- Many African American women served as nurses, but could only treat African American soldiers.
- There were fighter squadrons of African-American-only pilots.

Similarly, in the workplace:
- African American workers generally earned half of what white workers did.
- In 1942, at the Packard electronics company, 3,000 white workers walked out when three African American workers had their jobs upgraded.

There were race riots in 47 cities during the war, the worst of which was in Detroit during June–July 1943. The war years, however, did see some progress.
- As the war developed, racially integrated units became more commonplace because General Eisenhower was a supporter of them. Such units performed with distinction at the Battle of the Bulge in December 1944 (see page 124).
- The number of African American officers greatly increased.
- The war gave African Americans the opportunity to press for equality of civil rights. The African American press set up the 'Double V' campaign. This campaign pushed President Roosevelt into action. In 1941 he issued Executive Order 8802 which ordered employers on defence work to end discrimination. The Fair Employment Practices Committee was set up to investigate violations of this Order.
- In 1942 African American leaders set up the Congress of Racial Equality (CORE).
- Membership of the National Association for the Advancement of Colored People (NAACP) increased tenfold between 1940 and 1946.

Racism in the 1950s

Most southern states fully enforced the **Jim Crow** laws which **segregated** everyday facilities such as parks, buses and schools. African Americans had officially been given the vote in the early years of the twentieth century but violence often prevented them from actually voting. In the South, white teachers earned 30 per cent more than African American teachers. The best universities were closed to African American people.

Progress in education

For decades it had been legal in the USA for states to have separate schools for African American and white children. Schools for African American children were always less well equipped.

The NAACP and the African American **civil rights** lawyer Thurgood Marshall brought a series of complaints about segregated schools in the 1940s. Judge Julius Waring ruled that states had to provide equal education for African American and white students but said nothing about integration.

Brown v. Topeka Board of Education

The *Brown v. Board of Education of Topeka* case of 1954 showed further progress in education. In 1952 the NAACP brought a court case against the Board of Education of Topeka in Kansas on behalf of an African American student, Linda Brown, who had to walk a considerable distance to get to school because she was not allowed to attend the whites-only school near her home. In May 1954 Chief Justice Earl Warren ruled in favour of Brown and stated that segregated education could not be equal because African American students had inferior facilities. He ordered the southern states to set up integrated schools 'with all deliberate speed'.

Challenging inequality through the legal system was the method favoured by the NAACP civil rights campaigners. They took an individual case all the way to the Supreme Court, which decided in their favour, thus forcing the states to act.

Little Rock

This method was also used at Little Rock in Arkansas, in one of the most important developments in the civil rights movement.

Arkansas had not yet introduced integrated education, but in 1957 the Supreme Court ordered the Governor, Orval Faubus, to let nine African American students attend a white school in Little Rock. Faubus brought out state troops to stop them, insisting he was using the troops to protect the children. Faubus only backed down when President Eisenhower sent federal troops to protect the students.

The Montgomery Bus Boycott

This took place in Montgomery, Alabama, in 1955 and is normally seen as the beginning of the civil rights movement.

- In Montgomery a local law stated that African Americans had to sit on the back seats of buses and had to give up those seats if white people wanted them.
- Rosa Parks, an NAACP activist, refused to give up her seat and was arrested and convicted of breaking the bus laws.
- Local civil rights activists set up the Montgomery Improvement Association (MIA), led by Martin Luther King. They boycotted the buses and organised private transport for people. This was a great success and the first example of non-violent direct action. It showed how powerful African American people could be if they worked together.
- Civil rights lawyers fought Rosa Parks' case in court. In December 1956 the Supreme Court declared Montgomery's bus laws illegal.

This was the beginning of non-violent mass protests by the civil rights movement.

Key terms

Jim Crow: the name Jim Crow was made popular by a white American comedian who made fun of African Americans. Originally, Jim Crow was a character in an old song. This name became linked to the southern lakes ensuring that African American people remained inferior.

Segregation: keeping a group separate from the rest of society, usually on the basis of race or religion. Segregation was seen in separate schools, transport and housing.

Civil rights: legal rights, such as freedom of speech and the right to a fair trial. Most African Americans lacked these basic rights in the 1950s.

Exam tip Students often confuse *Brown v. Topeka Board of Education* and Little Rock. Ensure you are clear about the differences between these two key events.

Exam tip *Brown v. Topeka Board of Education*, Little Rock and the Montgomery Bus Boycott are very popular exam topics. Ensure you revise these thoroughly.

Progress, 1958–62

The civil rights movement gathered pace in the late 1950s and early 1960s due mainly to the leadership of Martin Luther King.

Direct action gathers pace

In the winter of 1959–60 civil rights groups stepped up their campaigns.

- They organised marches, demonstrations and boycotts to end segregation in public places. In February 1960 in Nashville, Tennessee, 500 students organised sit-ins in restaurants, libraries and churches. Their college expelled them but then backed down when 400 teachers threatened to resign. By May 1960 the town had been desegregated.
- In May 1961 both white and African American members of the Congress of Racial Equality (CORE) began a form of protest known as 'freedom rides' in the southern states. They deliberately rode on buses run by companies that were ignoring laws banning segregation. They faced much violence and opposition. By September, 70,000 students had taken part and 3,600 had been arrested.

Martin Luther King

King became the leading figure in the civil rights movement until his assassination in 1968. He believed passionately in non-violent protest and favoured actions such as the bus boycott and sit-ins. He won increased support for the civil rights movement by appealing to students. From this emerged, in April 1960, the Student Non-violent Co-ordinating Committee (SNCC). Many SNCC workers dropped out of their studies to work full time in those areas that were most resistant to integration.

In the summer of 1961 the main civil rights groups – SNCC, CORE and NAACP – met with the Attorney-General, Robert Kennedy, brother of the new president, John F. Kennedy. Together they devised the Voter Education Project, which aimed to get more African American people registered to vote.

> ### Comment
> *The freedom riders faced much opposition from the Ku Klux Klan who frequently attacked the riders but were rarely prosecuted by the local police. During one of the early freedom rides in Alabama in May 1961, one of the buses was firebombed outside Anniston. As the bus burned, the mob held the doors shut, intent on burning the riders to death. However, an exploding petrol tank forced the mob to flee and enabled the riders to escape – but only after they had been viciously beaten.*

> ### Comment
> *Martin Luther King did not invent the tactic of direct action. This had developed as a result of key education and transport cases of the 1950s and early 1960s. He did, however, provide national leadership for such action and ensured massive publicity for the cause of civil rights within and beyond the USA.*

Revision tasks

1 List four ways African Americans were treated as second-class citizens in the 1950s.

2 Make a copy of the table below. Complete it using the information from this section.

Dispute	Reason for dispute	Court decision	Importance
Brown v Topeka			
Little Rock			
Montgomery bus boycott			

3 Draw a timeline to show the progress made from 1959–61 in the civil rights campaign.

4

SOURCE 2 A sit-in at a 'whites only' lunch counter in Jackson, Mississippi, June 1963.

Exam tip: q4 You need to explain:
- what the source is suggesting
- what message it is trying to get across
- its purpose. What is it trying to make people think or do?

Why do you think Source 2 was widely publicised? Explain your answer using details from the source and your own knowledge.

12.3 Changes in the civil rights movement, 1963–70

Although Martin Luther King continued to dominate the civil rights movement, there was increasing support for more extreme methods such as those of the Black Power movement.

The peace marches

- In April 1963 King organised a march on Birmingham, Alabama, as the city had still not been desegregated. The aim of the march was to turn national attention on Birmingham and expose its policies. Police Chief Bull Connor ordered police and fire officers to turn dogs and fire hoses on the peaceful protesters. The police arrested over 1,000 protesters, including King. King's tactics worked, as President Kennedy forced Governor George Wallace to release the prisoners and desegregate Birmingham.
- In August 1963 King staged his most high-profile event. Over 200,000 African Americans and 50,000 white Americans marched together to Washington to pressure Kennedy to introduce a civil rights bill. There was no trouble and King gave his famous 'I have a dream' speech.

Civil rights legislation

The Civil Rights Bill was introduced by President Kennedy but was not passed before his assassination in November 1963.

Civil Rights Act

In November 1963 Kennedy was assassinated. His successor, Lyndon Johnson, was just as committed to civil rights. On 2 July 1964 he signed the Civil Rights Act. The Act made it illegal for local government to discriminate in areas such as housing and employment. The summer of 1964 was known as the 'freedom summer'. King and the SNCC continued to encourage African Americans to register to vote. In the twenty months that followed the Civil Rights Act, 430,000 African Americans registered to vote.

King's campaigns, 1965–68

King continued to target areas where discrimination was worst. In 1965 he organised a march through Selma, Alabama, which had a notoriously racist sheriff called Jim Clark, to protest against the violence being used to stop African American voters from registering. The authorities banned the march but 600 people went ahead and were brutally attacked. The media called it 'Bloody Sunday'. King organised a second march but compromised with the authorities by turning back after a certain distance. This lost King the support of the more radical African American activists, but nevertheless helped President Johnson to push through a Voting Rights Bill in 1965 which finally became law in 1968. The Act allowed government agents to inspect voting procedures to make sure that they were taking place properly. It also ended the literacy tests that voters had previously had to complete before they voted. After 1965 five major cities had African American mayors.

In April 1968 King was assassinated, probably by a hired killer.

Malcolm X and Black Power

African American nationalism became more popular in the 1960s and won much support.

Reasons

Most African American nationalists rejected the non-violence of the civil rights movement. They felt violence was justified to achieve full equality. Some even wanted complete separation from the rest of the USA. One of the groups that called for this was the Nation of Islam, led by Elijah Mohammad. This group attracted high-profile figures such as the boxer Cassius Clay (later known as Muhammad Ali).

Malcolm X

One member of the Nation of Islam was Malcolm Little, better known as Malcolm X. He was bitterly critical of King's methods and believed the civil rights movement held African American people back. He wanted to see African Americans rise up and use force if necessary to set up their own separate state in the USA. He was assassinated in 1965.

Just before his death Malcolm X visited Mecca in the Middle East and was impressed with the way in which people from different races mixed well together. On his return to the USA he moved towards King's idea of an integrated society.

> **Exam tip** Malcolm X was not a Black Power leader. He died before the movement was set up.

Black Power

- The SNCC became more radical when the African American student Stokely Carmichael was elected chairman in 1966. He talked of 'Black Power' and criticised King.
- An even more radical group was the Black Panthers. They had around 2,000 members and were a political party and a small private army. They believed that African Americans should arm themselves and force white Americans to give them equal rights. They clashed many times with the police, killing nine police officers between 1967 and 1969.

Between 1965 and 1967 American cities suffered a wave of race riots.
- This was largely due to poor relations between the police, who were mainly white, and African American people. Many African American working-class people did not feel they got the same protection from crime as white people.
- Many African American rioters were influenced by the radical African American nationalists.

● Others joined the riots because of their frustration with the way they were treated in the USA.

The most serious riots were in the Watts area of Los Angeles in August 1965 and in Detroit in July 1967.

Revision tasks

1 Make a copy of the following table. Use information from this section to explain the part played by each individual in the civil rights campaign of the 1960s.

Individual	Part played
Martin Luther King	
Elijah Mohammad	
Malcolm X	
Stokely Carmichael	

2 Using a few key words explain the reasons for:
a) the Black Power movement
b) the race riots in the USA, 1965–67.

3

SOURCE 3   A photograph showing the civil rights march on Washington DC, 1963.

How useful is Source 3 as evidence of the methods used by Martin Luther King to campaign for civil rights in the 1960s?

Exam tip For revision task 3 you need to evaluate:
● what is useful about what the source shows and suggests about King's methods
● the limitations in what it shows and suggests, bringing in your own contextual knowledge of King's methods and the march
● what is useful and what are the limitations of the purpose of the photograph; of why it was taken?

12.4 Other protest movements of the 1960s

The campaign for African American civil rights encouraged other protest movements including those campaigning for women's rights and the student movement.

The reasons for the student movement

The 1960s was a decade of social unrest and this spread to the USA's youth, especially in universities and colleges. Student protest emerged for several reasons.

- Students were deeply involved in the African American civil rights campaign and also the women's movement. Idealistic young students were appalled at the injustices experienced by African American people.
- The death of President Kennedy in 1963 came as a great shock to the American people, especially the young who had been inspired by his brief presidency.
- The war in Vietnam united student protest. Half a million young Americans were fighting in a war that was very unpopular with students. The anti-war protests reached a peak between 1968 and 1970.
- The 1960s saw the pop music explosion and the popularity of the protest singer. This was epitomised by the singer/songwriter Bob Dylan whose lyrics attacked war and racism.
- The 1960s was also a time of student unrest across the world.

Key features of the student movement

There were many different groups involved in student protest. One of the main organisations was Students for a Democratic Society, set up in 1959. It aimed to get more say for students in how their colleges and universities were run and had 100,000 members by the end of the 1960s.

- In 1964 radical students in many colleges organised rallies and marches to support the civil rights campaign. They tried to expose racism in their own colleges. Some universities tried to ban their protests. The students responded with a Free Speech Movement. Student groups also backed campaigns for nuclear disarmament and criticised US involvement in South America.
- During the first half of 1968 there were over 100 demonstrations against the Vietnam War involving 40,000 students. Anti-war demonstrations often ended in violent clashes with the police. The worst incident came in 1970 at Kent State University, Ohio, where students organised a demonstration against President Nixon's decision to invade Cambodia. The National Guards panicked and fired on the students, killing four.
- Some young people took up an entirely different kind of protest. They 'dropped out' and became hippies. They opted out of the society their parents had created. They decided not to work or study. They grew their hair long, talked of peace and love, and experimented with sex and drugs.

Exam tip Remember that the student movement is not just about protests against the Vietnam War.

The women's movement

This was not one single organisation but thousands of different groups all with similar aims – to raise the status of women and end discrimination against women in all areas of life.

Reasons for movement

- In 1963 Betty Freidan wrote a best-seller called *The Feminine Mystique*. This was her term for a set of ideas that said that women's happiness came from being wives and mothers. Freidan challenged this notion, insisting that many married women needed employment to avoid frustration and boredom. She wrote of hundreds of college-educated women who felt little better than domestic servants.

Comment

Women's attitudes also changed because of the introduction of the contraceptive pill in 1960. This changed women's attitudes to sexual relations and gave them much greater independence and control of their lives.

- Inequality in employment: the number of women in employment had continued to increase in the years after the Second World War, but there were problems. Eleanor Roosevelt, the widow of President Roosevelt, made an important contribution to the women's movement when, in 1960, she set up a commission to investigate the status of women at work. When it reported in 1963 it found that 93 per cent of company managers and 88 per cent of technical workers were men and only 4 per cent of lawyers and 7 per cent of doctors were female. Work for women was overwhelmingly low paid, with many earning only 50 per cent of the wages of men for doing the same job.

Key features

Women's rights received a boost from the Federal Government, which passed a number of important measures, and from the Supreme Court. In 1963 the Equal Pay Act required employers to pay women the same as men for the same work. This, however, did not stop discrimination against female employment.

The following year the Civil Rights Act made it illegal to discriminate on grounds of gender. In 1972 the Educational Amendment Act outlawed sex discrimination in education, and courses had to be rewritten to ensure that gender stereotyping did not occur in the curriculum. In 1973 the Supreme Court's ruling in the *Roe v Wade* case made abortion legal.

Women's organisations

Various organisations emerged in the 1960s.

- In 1966 Betty Freidan set up the National Organisation for Women (NOW) which had 40,000 members by the early 1970s. It co-operated with a wide range of women's movements, such as the National Women's Caucus and the Women's Campaign Fund. It used similar tactics to the civil rights movement, campaigning in the streets of American cities and challenging discrimination in court. NOW, however, was not an extreme organisation and still believed in traditional families and marriage.
- In contrast, there were younger feminists with more radical aims and different methods. They became known as the Women's Liberation Movement (Women's Lib). They used more extreme methods to get across their views, such as bra-burning, since bras were seen as a symbol of male domination. In 1968 radical women picketed the Miss World beauty contest in Atlantic City. They said that the contest treated women like objects rather than women. To make their point, they crowned a sheep as Miss World.

What did the women's movement achieve?

The women's movement achieved much publicity and support, with several important laws passed. However, there were limitations.

- Some support was lost because of the extreme methods of the Women's Lib Movement which some believed ridicules the position of women.
- Anti-feminist organisations were set up, with the most famous, STOP ERA, led by Phylis Schafly. ERA stood for Equality Rights Amendment, which was a proposal to amend the US Constitution to outlaw sex discrimination. Schafly led a successful campaign to prevent it becoming law as late at the 1980s.
- Despite legislation, few women had achieved top posts in Congress, business or industry by the end of the 1970s.

Exam tip Students often give vague, generalised answers about the women's movement. Ensure you have precise knowledge of why it emerged, its key features and importance.

Comment

We tend to look at the protest movements of the 1960s separately. This does not give us a real idea of what was happening. Many individuals were not campaigning only for women's rights, or an end to the war in Vietnam or for civil rights. They supported several or all of these movements. In some respects protest itself became fashionable, especially amongst the young, heavily influenced by protest singers such as Bob Dylan.

Revision tasks

1 Make a copy of the following table and use the information from this section to complete it.

	Reasons for	Key features	Importance of
Student movement			
Women's movement			

2

SOURCE 4

From *The Feminine Mystique*, by Betty Friedan, 1963.

As the American woman made beds, shopped for groceries, matched slipcover material, ate peanut butter sandwiches with her children, chauffeured Cub Scouts and Brownies, lay beside her husband at night, she was afraid to ask even herself the question: 'Is this all?'

How reliable is Source 4 as a view of women in US society in the early 1960s?

Exam tip: q2 You need to evaluate:
- what is reliable about what the source shows and suggests about the position of women compared to your knowledge of women in the USA in the 1960s
- the limitations in what it shows and suggests, bringing in your own contextual knowledge of the 1960s
- what is reliable and unreliable about who wrote the book and its purpose.

Key content

You need to have a good working knowledge of the following areas:

- the reasons for the Red Scare, including the Cold War and developments in the USA
- the key features of McCarthyism and why it declined
- *Brown v. Topeka Board of Education*, Little Rock and the Montgomery Bus Boycott
- the leadership and methods of Martin Luther King
- sit-ins and freedom riders of the early 1960s
- the civil rights marches of 1963 and the 'freedom summer'
- civil rights legislation of the 1960s
- Malcolm X, Black Power and the inner-city riots
- reasons for and key features of the student movement
- reasons for, key features of and importance of the women's movement.